Redeemed by Accident

Joseph Ricky Reynolds

Ideas into Books® W E S T V I E W
Kingston Springs, Tennessee

Ideas into Books®
W E S T V I E W
P.O. Box 605
Kingston Springs, TN 37082
www.publishedbywestview.com

ISBN 978-1-62880-283-2

First edition, November 2023

Front cover photo and design by Rachel Wood, Graphic Designer

Digitally printed worldwide on acid free paper.

Acknowledgements

I would like to thank all those who have made this book possible.

My wife, Diane, for all of her hard work. For the countless hours of typing while trying to decipher my handwriting.

A special thanks to Kennedy Mook, my granddaughter, an 11th grade English teacher in Chattanooga, Tennessee, for all of her hard work in getting this work ready to publish.

A special thanks to my daughters, Michelle, Crystal, and Misti, who are the light of our lives. Thank you for your encouragement while I was endeavoring to write this book.

To my grandchildren who have encouraged me to tell my story: Joey, Kennedy, Tyler, Brian, Bailey, Carson, Andrew and Vada.

Table Of Contents

Introduction

I'm running at full speed, diving into the water. I have hit bottom with a tremendous force. My face is buried in the silt and debris at the bottom of the lake. I can remember my arms being outstretched. I'm stunned and shocked by the sudden impact. I somehow have the constitution to hold my breath. Barely conscious, I can feel myself being pulled or dragged toward the shoreline.

My friends are gathered around me. I can see them now. They are distraught and confused; they're also trying to understand what's happening. I can remember looking up and seeing their faces. The confusion and terror in their eyes. I remember telling them that I would be okay. I'm just stunned. That's when I made a crucial mistake. I tried to sit up. When I attempted to raise a few inches, I felt as though a thousand sharp needles were pricking my body all over. Piercing needles of severe pain and agony. That's when I passed out for the second time.

*W*ith pen in hand, I feel like something is calling me to tell my story. I believe all of us have experiences in life that help mold and shape us into what God wants us to be. I'm hoping that the reader can relate and say to themselves, "You know what, I know exactly where he's coming from." To use a modern phrase that someone said to me recently, "I'm picking up what you're putting down." At the time of this writing, I was three score and ten years old. The Psalmist wrote that a man's lifespan was to be approximately 70 years. Out of my 70 years, I feel that at least 55 of those years have been borrowed time. In 1969 a very serious accident paralyzed me from my chest down. That warm spring day changed the course of my life forever. It was the worst day of my life, but also the best day of my life. The day that I was Redeemed, by accident.

Chapter 1

The Old Homeplace

*I*t's the late '50s and I am now almost seven years old. I have awakened and it's very cold in the rear corner bedroom of that old six-room house. Five rooms and a bath. The old house was originally built with just four rooms and a path that led to an old outhouse out back. My father added an extra bedroom and a bathroom inside as the family began to grow. The bedroom that two of my older brothers and I shared was very small. An old full-size bed with a lumpy mattress. One window with plain rail sashes that at times would allow fine sifting snow that was accompanied by high winds, to press its way through the cracks and crevices. The snow would sometimes settle on our blankets and quilts that were on our beds. I could tell by the temperature in the room that it was going to be very cold outside. No joke, I can stick my head out from under the covers and see my breath as I lay here dreading getting out of bed.

My ears are tuned to the movements in the house. I'm listening to the squeak of the old metal springs on my mother and father's bed. The squeaks of the old one-by-four tongue and groove flooring in my parent's bedroom. As I heard these things I knew that my mother and father were rising to start their day.

In the center of the living room was an old warm morning, wood-burning stove. The black stove pipe, about six inches in diameter, protruded from the rear of that old heater and climbed toward the ceiling. It then made a ninety-degree turn into a brick chimney that my father built with his own hands. That old stove became the hero on many cold winter days and nights. During the early morning hours, the heat had retreated as the fire had burned down.

My mother, on most mornings, would be the one who would open the door of that old stove and bring it back to life. I could hear the door open and then a poker would scratch and clang against the sides. Mama would search for live coals that were hiding beneath the ashes. I can hear the breaking of the kindling gathered and stored to ignite a new flame. This would bring heat and comfort to the old living room that had been overcome with the frosty air of the night. There was always a pan of water on top of the heater to hold the dust down. Don't get me wrong, this was a nice heater. With the latest technology, a damper is built into the door. A beautiful steel mesh jacket that covered the firebox. Not unsightly at all, but very modern for the day. My mother was proud of that heater because she had bought and paid for it in monthly installments.

It's the room in the house where my family gathers early in the morning and the evening. An old linoleum rug that doesn't cover the entire floor. The outside edges of the floor are one-by-four tongue and groove that has been painted. Knotty pine paneling on the walls. A black and white TV on legs, with rabbit ears, an old couch, and some random chairs, one of those chairs was my father's favorite. My father would sit in his chair and he would sometimes even pay us kids a nickel to rub his feet.

I'll climb out of bed in a few minutes. My brothers, Jr, who is the oldest, and Kenneth, who is older than me, but only by fifteen months, shared a bedroom. As flames start to fuel the fire, the metal begins to expand and pop and the heater starts to drive the cold from the room. My brothers and I would then head into the living room where my mother was preparing to start the day and get the family in motion.

We're out of bed. The old house is getting cozy. The new-found heat that the old stove is beginning to puff out, is warming up the corners of the old place. Is that sausage I smell? Man, it's almost time to eat—eggs frying and crackling with an occasional pop. Be careful, Mama, that hurts. Toast, laying on the oven rack, turning golden and brown with little clumps of butter, melting and mostly disappearing beneath the surface of that Colonial bread. I know it was Colonial bread because my father would not buy any other brand, he was so picky. The old metal coffee pot on the stove begins to percolate a song as the smell of coffee begins to permeate throughout the house.

I can see my daddy coming to the table. Not a large man, maybe a hundred and seventy pounds. Always clean shaven, sitting at the head of the table, because that's where fathers were supposed to sit. One egg over medium, two sausage patties, a piece of toast, a coffee with cream and sugar. Before we would eat, our father would bow his head and whisper a few words of thanks and start eating.

My father was facing a hard day. A house to be built, a footing to be dug, a roof to be put on. Construction was his life and his livelihood, it's a funny thing. The house that he's building today is much tighter than the house that we live in. But what's the old saying? A mechanic's car always needs work, a painter's house always needs painting, a roofer's house may leak, and so on. This old house was our home. My mother's love was very strong. Her faith was unshakable. Although my father seldom expressed his love for us, he proved it every day. My father's determination to keep a roof over our head, and food on our table, proved his love for us. He was not what I would call an affectionate man. Only one time in my life can I remember him telling me, or any of my siblings, that he loved us, but we knew he did.

As time passed, there were three brothers and a little sister. The little sister, Janice, who was the apple of my father's eye, the little jewel, the princess. Believe it or not, two more boys would come along a little later.

The school bus is coming! Get dressed. Where are your shoes? Mama, is this the only shirt I've got clean? My pants have a hole in them. I forgot to polish my shoes. Hurry up! I can hear the bus. You see this was possible because the road was gravel, not limestone, but gravel that the county had harvested from creek beds and spread with an old road grader. We would sit on the front porch and punch each other and say, "I'm the one who heard it first. That's the bus coming," "Is not," "Is too. I can tell! Listen, he just changed gears and turned in on our road. " The gravel road. I can still remember our bus number was 42. I can't remember the driver's name, but I can remember the peach tree switch that he kept hanging above the driver's seat. The switch was a constant reminder for the students to behave. I can't remember him ever having to take that switch down from its perch.

Chapter 2

Siblings

You see, I'm the middle child. My older brothers would get on my nerves. My brother Junior is named after my father (Arthur Turner Reynolds, Jr). He's smart and hardworking, and he was always trying to boss my brother Kenneth and me around. We would tell him, "We don't have to listen to you." He would say to us, "Tie your shoes." "I don't have to!" "We've got to cut wood for the stove." "You can't make me!" Nevertheless, our oldest brother always kept us in line.

He thinks he's grown because Daddy lets him drive now; he's almost 16, and I'm just 12. My brother, Kenneth, is somewhere in between. I can remember a time when our parents weren't home and Kenneth decided to take his motorcycle apart and paint it. He decided to do that on our Mother's new hardwood floor. After he was finished you could see the outline of every part that he had painted. Needless to say, our mother wasn't very happy when she came home. We were famous for doing things when Mama and Daddy weren't home. For example, Jr decided to take Daddy's 1963 Mercury Meteor out for a joy ride on the old country road. We got to the end of the road and needing to turn around, he pulled in beside Mr. Jim's old tobacco barn. As he began to back out and he couldn't see, he decided to open the driver's door and look back. Not seeing the stump he hung the driver's door and almost pulled it off. Our father wasn't very happy with us that day.

*J*r would let us ride to the old country store, that is if we would act right. Now acting right, according to him, went something like this. Let me share. Keep your feet out of the seats. Don't slam the car door. Stop fighting over whose riding shotgun. (In case you don't know what that means, I'll explain. The one who cried shotgun got to ride in the front seat, passenger side. Off to the store — A loaf of bread, Colonial, a half a gallon of milk, a six-pack. Don't get alarmed, the six-pack included a Dr. Pepper for Mama for sure and an Almond Joy. The rest of the order varied, an RC cola, a Nehi grape, an Orange Crush, a small Coke for Daddy. A Zero candy bar, a Zag Nut, and maybe a Baby Ruth. After slamming that old screen door to the country store, we head out by the old worn church pew setting on the store porch. Past the farmers and the loafers who are drinking their RC Colas and eating Moon Pies. Hollering as we get into the car," We'll bring your bottles back." Sure!!! Uh-oh. We forgot something. We need to get a dollar's worth of gas. Then it's back down that gravel road.

I experienced many wonderful times living in the country, and the smells of the seasons. Springtime and summer were my favorite times. The eerie sounds of the night, the sounds of the Whip-poor-wills and the Bobwhites. There's a deer in the tree line. The rippling streams, the wind whistling through the trees, the lightning bugs, the June bugs, and the occasional scream of a Bobcat. I don't want to leave out the tumble bugs, as I follow them down the road that I have made for my little toy cars. Cars and trucks that my mama bought me at the five and dime store in Ashland City.

My brother Kenneth and I were very close. We played in the woods together quite often. We had discovered that you could smoke grapevines. My father caught us doing this one time and told us that we would suck a flame down our throat. I don't think we ever sucked a flame down our throat but I do remember getting a mouth full of ants on a few occasions. But even that didn't stop us from smoking grapevines. We would cut the larger grapevines and would swing from tree to tree like Tarzan.

We played in the creek and swam in Cheatham Lake, occasionally borrowing someone's boat that was tied to a tree on the shore. We did this one time and the man was waiting on us when we came back and he said, "Boys, are y'all finished with my boat?"

I have many memories of living in the country. Going hunting with my daddy's old 16-gauge, Iver Johnson Shotgun that he kept hanging above the front door of the old house. I would get a chair and stand on it, to retrieve the shotgun from the homemade gun rack; that's when I admired my Father's ingenuity. The gun rack was made from a limb about the size of a quarter. It was cut at the fork, kinda like making a slingshot. This was then nailed to the knotty pine paneling on the wall above the door. I don't know the whereabouts of that old gun, but hopefully, it's somewhere, hanging above a door.

Chapter 3

The Old Walnut House

I was so fortunate as a child, and even into my teenage years, to have grandparents on both sides of the family. My mother and my father's parents were very much active in our young lives.

My mother's side of the family, the Batsons, Granddaddy Batson, (nicknamed Pumpkin to all his friends), and my Grandmama Batson, (Lydia Mai), were both good-hearted and kind. But on occasion, my grandfather's disciplinary tactics would be considered quite abusive today. Sitting at the dinner table one day while my granddaddy was saying Grace over our meal, I asked my Uncle Jackie, "Did you see that big old rat out by the cistern?" Granddaddy said, "Stick, (this was the nickname my granddaddy called me) go get me a switch," but I cried my way out of that one. His methods of discipline were pretty common and were used by parents of the World War II generation. I heard quite a bit about the use of a peach tree limb to improve the behavior of his children.

My Granddaddy Batson was an entrepreneur even before anyone knew what the word meant. Any type of business that was honest, he would try. He raised pigs and chickens. He grew butter beans, green beans, corn, sugar cane, and all sorts of garden vegetables that could be sold from the back of his old Chevrolet pickup (an early 50s model, I believe).

His most interesting business endeavor that I can remember, and even helped with some, was his black walnut business. That's right, I said black walnut business. In Tennessee. Years ago, the countryside was full of black walnut trees. These walnuts grew to the size of tennis balls and smaller when they were still in the hull. After the walnuts fell from the trees in the fall, my grandfather and family would gather them up. They would then move them to a designated area for what I call the dehulling. The outer layer of the walnut would rot or deteriorate, and then they could be removed to reveal the black hard shell that protects the kernel inside.

My grandfather had the most innovative way of doing this particular step. He simply ran over them with his old pickup truck. They were then cracked to harvest the kernel inside. After the process of dehulling, they were brought into what was known, at least to us, as the Old Walnut House.

The Old Walnut House was an old building with a low ceiling and a low-pitched roof. A place designed to take the walnuts to the next step in the process. I have a memory of my Uncle Bud cracking the walnuts so that the kernels could be removed. The kernels were picked through to discard the bad and separate the good, this process was done by the Batson girls.

I can still see my mama, Lena, Frances, Aline, and Grandmama Batson, sitting at the table, sorting the beautiful kernels from the rejects. The kernels were then hand-delivered to an ice cream factory in Nashville to make delicious black walnut ice cream.

I hope I have painted a mental portrait of my Granddaddy Batson. Let me cap it off with this: He was a hard worker, a godly man, a strict disciplinarian, a devoted husband, very strong physically, and faithful to the end.

There's simply not enough time or pages to give him the respect and recognition that he deserves. I am 70 years old now, and I still think about him quite often. I pray that I will be able to influence and inspire someone the way that he inspired me and others.

Living across the Holler from my grandparents and my aunts and uncles are some of my fondest memories. My brothers and I would walk an old path, down the hill, occasionally stopping for a sip of water at the old spring. We would then climb the old path, back up the hill, toward our old house, sitting next to the gravel road. Granddaddy would go to Nashville and pick up boxes of shoes and bring them home. He would call my mama and tell her to bring the boys over to pick them out a pair of, not new shoes, but new to us. My granddaddy had an old shoe last and when the soles of the shoes would wear out, he would cut up automobile tires and use that to make new soles. I have heard the story told about Uncle Donnie, who got a new pair and they were too big so Granddaddy cut them off and used hog rings to close the toes.

He would drive his old truck to Nashville and buy day-old bread. He would bring it home and pick out the freshest to share with his family and feed the rest of it to his hogs. I was told this story by an old gentleman in Ashland City, TN. He said he was hitchhiking one day and my granddaddy picked him up. He said when he got in the truck Granddaddy was telling him about the Lord. He said he started telling him about the Holy Go. The old gentleman misunderstood. Granddaddy was telling him about the Holy Ghost (The Spirit of God).

My grandparents also ran a little country store. I have memories of the surrounding neighbors coming there to buy groceries. Bits and pieces of that old building, still to this day, are preserved on the property where Granddaddy and Grandmama Batson lived. This property is located between Ashland City and Charlotte, TN on Pumpkin Ave.

My grandmama Batson—boy! Could she cook? Mmm. Mmm. Mmm.

You see, meals in the Batson kitchen were not quite the same as meals in my family's kitchen. I told you about sausage and eggs at my house, but Grandmama's house was a different story. My grandparents were not coffee drinkers. The go-to breakfast drink was cocoa, made on top of the stove in a pan with a handle and poured into a cup. I remember breakfast being fried bologna, preserves, sorghum molasses, and biscuits, and Grandmama would also fry up potatoes. Remember I told you my grandfather was a Godly man, so coffee was a no-no, because of the caffeine. I'll always remember the German chocolate cake. I also remember a cake that she called "Pudding" with chocolate syrup. The coconut pie was so delicious. Even to this day, everyone tries to duplicate it, although I must say that my cousin, Melissa, has come close to making the pie that I can remember as a child.

Speaking of my granddaddy being a Godly man, I can remember the story of the day that a mule kicked my Uncle Bud in the head. My Granddaddy poured kerosene on my uncle's head, mashed it together, and prayed for him and the Lord closed the wound. Later on, my Uncle Bud testified about this miracle on many occasions.

Before I move to another chapter, I would like to include in this story the fact that country folks are a lot smarter than typical city slickers give us credit. As I've already said, we attended school regularly. The first school I attended was small, in the community of Bellsburg. I can remember a time when I wanted to impress a pretty girl in my classroom, so I decided that eating a bar of soap would be a good idea. I'm not quite sure if my blowing bubbles impressed her or not. The best I can remember, I learned this trick from Alfalfa, who was one of the little rascals. Alfalfa was always in the mood for love!!!

*W*e stayed abreast of community affairs. Even though we did not have Facebook, Twitter, or Instagram, we knew everybody's business. We had what was called a party line. Ma Bell was helping the community connect long before the Internet. I feel like I've left you hanging, so I need to explain how this all worked. We were modern people who had a telephone, hardwired from the telephone pole, not quite green acres, but close. You may want to look that up on the web, but with this system, there were several people on the same line. That's why it was called a party line. Each home or family had a different ring, this way they would know just when the call was for them. My grandparents' ring was two very short rings like this "ring ring." Ain't that something? You may ask, how is information shared? I'll tell you, everyone on the same party line could hear conversations from their neighbors. So if you picked up the receiver to make a call, someone could already be talking on that line. Oops. Sorry. Didn't mean to pick up. Of course, no one would listen very long. Bits and pieces of conversations between neighbors usually kept everyone informed of community affairs and gossip. It was kind of like Facebook today without the photos. Country folks were smart and well-informed. Ya hear?

Chapter 4

City Slickers

To borrow a line from history, "It was the best of times. It was the worst of times."

My father's construction business began to grow, so we moved to the city of Clarksville, Tennessee, in 1960. Population approximately 23,000. Daddy is doing business, connections are being made, and subdivisions are being developed.

Mama has a new house, no more wood stoves. A brick house with a full basement and a carport, 3 bedrooms, 1 ½ baths on Rosewood Drive in Clarksville. Oh boy—Things are looking up for our little family. We are starting in a new school with all of us kids who were of school age, now going to school together. This was Roosevelt Elementary School, located on 41A. The Clarksville Montgomery County Bus Depot is standing there now. Roosevelt went from first through the eighth grade. Mr. Carlton Robbins was our principal. I can remember going to Roosevelt in the 2nd, 3rd, and 4th, and then in the 5th grade. I can remember my teacher's name was Mrs. Weakley in the 5th grade. It was in this class at Roosevelt that I met the love of my life, my future wife. But I didn't know it then.

As I have mentioned, my father's construction business was beginning to take off. He was building houses right and left. But as many men do when success starts to come their way, especially those who never had much, they go on spending sprees. I remember all of a sudden, we had more than one telephone in the house, Ceramic tile bathrooms, a brick home with hardwood in most of the home, and wall-to-wall carpet in the formal living room. That living room was off-limits unless company came.

My father started dressing sharp. I can remember his black and white slippers that I thought were so sharp. Nowadays, those slippers would be cool, but then they were sharp. We used phrases like "man, that's a sharp truck or car, or boat." We thought we had it all, or at least it seemed that way. We even had a family pet, a dog named Rusty. I can remember a funny story about Rusty. One time a supplier brought my father a Christmas present. It was a bottle of whiskey. My mother in anger had taken it behind our home and poured it out. I guess Rusty didn't know any better so he just lapped it up. Watching our family pet stagger around in the backyard gave a new meaning to the phrase, *Drunk as a dog.*

All of a sudden, a brand-new Cadillac sat on the paved driveway. A new pickup truck. Yeah, you may have guessed it—a new boat and trailer, which was unbelievable. We have never had anything like this before.

What happened next was a gradual migration toward materialism that our family had never experienced. Even my dear sweet country girl Mama began to enjoy the finer things in life. She started wearing new fashions, but not jewelry, not even a wedding band. Those things she avoided because she was brought up in a very strict, conservative household. But, a nice wristwatch was not out of the question.

The father that we would see every night while living in the country, all of a sudden began to disappear from our lives. The money was rolling in, and home life was prosperous, but something was happening in our little family that I didn't understand until many years later. My father was changing, but not for the better. His aloofness with us became more and more. He became more distant in our lives. I do remember a couple of rides in his new boat, or going to a job site with him.

There was a special Saturday night in which he took us to a stock car race. I can still visualize those loud, old cars going round and round on an old dirt track. While watching the race my father told my brothers and me to not leave the bleachers. He was going to the restroom area. But for some reason, I just had to follow him in that direction. I found him standing beside the restroom. It was the first time that I saw him smoking a cigarette, but he didn't see me. Something was changing in our family. I saw my father doing something that we had been taught all of our young lives not to do. But, smoking was nothing compared to what was to come.

It's late on Rosewood Drive. Everyone was in bed except my father. My father was out on one of his many binges. Sometime in the middle of the night, I woke up to a loud argument that was taking place in our den. It was my mama's voice, angrily fighting with my father. What's happening? This is so unusual. This was a new thing, the quiet of a peaceful night shattered by screaming and crying, those were my parents. But, I hardly recognized my father. He was messy, slouchy, belligerent—He was drunk! For many years to come late-night arguing would be a common occurrence.

You know—we have heard it said that "God works in mysterious ways." He is putting together a plan for our lives that will take years before it comes to fruition."

We didn't know it at the time, but my father was hiring a Pentecostal preacher, a bricklayer, to lay brick on many of his building projects. The message of the gospel was coming our way, but it will be a while coming. It was a message much deeper than religion. It was a message of Salvation that changed the direction in which our little family was going.

18

Chapter 5

Rise and Fall, Hard Times Have Just Begun

In the next few years, many things started to unfold in my family's little world — It was 1963, the year President John F. Kennedy was assassinated. In the 5th grade classroom at Roosevelt Elementary, as class was in session, I can still remember the effect that it had on me as a student, when one of the older classmates poked his head into the room and loudly announced the news of President Kennedy's assassination. My 5th-grade teacher, Mrs. Weakley, ran to the door, pushed the student outside, and shut the door. We students were then taken to the gym and a TV was brought in for us to watch the news story of the president being killed. It was a very sad time for our nation, and shocking to 5th graders who have not yet fully comprehended what had just happened.

This was the year that the last of the Reynolds' siblings were born, my little brother, Mark. My father was not home so my older brother, Jr, had to drive my mother to Memorial Hospital. It seemed that our happy little family was imploding. My father's newfound lifestyle was beginning to wreak havoc. Things began to go downhill when my father was arrested for a DWI, known more so today as a DUI, driving under the influence. After the DWI, his construction business began to suffer, his driver's license was taken away from him for six months and he had to hire drivers to take him from job site to job site.

He had several projects going on at this time. One project that he was in the middle of was an elementary school in an area of the city called New Providence. On this job site, he fell into an open ditch and broke his leg. He ended up in Memorial Hospital in Clarksville with double pneumonia. Things were falling apart at the seams, but he did not give up or leave people hanging. That wasn't in his nature. He finished his jobs, but in doing so destroyed all of the financial progress he had made in those short, three to four years.

*M*y father could have easily chosen to go bankrupt. With nothing else to do, my parents sold all of their newfound luxuries. The cars, trucks, houses, boats, etc. were sold to finish the jobs he had started and to pay off his existing debts. Our family packed up and moved back to the country.

Back into the old, cold, drafty house with the old wood stove. No thermostats on the walls. No more fancy cars or trucks. No paved driveways or manicured lawns. It was back to the dirt, gravel, and grind of country living. We as kids ended up going back to the Dickson County School system in Charlotte, Tennessee.

By this time, my father's drinking and what many called "Honky Tonking" had increased. The late-night arguments between my mother and father have become more frequent, almost every weekend.

My mother, the devoted homemaker, was doing a lot of praying and working to hold things together. At times—food was scarce. Bills were hard to pay. Work for my father was hit and miss. I heard him use the phrase often "Construction work is chicken one week and feathers the next." Instead of being a successful contractor, he was now picking up odd jobs and using his carpenter skills to occasionally frame a house for other builders.

About the time we were moving back to the country, there were five boys and one girl, a depressed father, and an angry, hurt mother who did not fully understand what was unfolding around them.

Things are starting to look up. A new opportunity for my father. A new job back in the city. So we packed up and headed back to town. We moved into a small three-bedroom, one-bath, rental house on Country Club Drive in Clarksville. We couldn't seem to get away from Clarksville. Even after moving back to the city, things were still complicated. In the midst of all of this, there was still the preacher.

Chapter 6

Wrong Direction

*D*uring the mid-1960s, America began to go through some drastic changes. The Vietnam War was raging. The youth of America were growing tired of our government shipping their friends off to a foreign land to die in a country that we knew very little about. Up until this time, we were convinced, as Americans, to always support the decisions of our leaders. But, the social climate in the country was experiencing winds of change.

The hippie generation was coming to light. LSD, marijuana, uppers, downers, anything that rebelled against society molded during the '50s and early '60s. The nuclear family era was starting to crumble. Racial inequalities were becoming more prevalent and were brought to light by several, especially Dr. Martin Luther King. Followers of his message were marching and fighting for equal rights for all.

Violence was erupting in the streets of the USA. On one hand, the hippies were preaching love and peace, along with Doctor King. On the other hand, there were those spewing protests with violence like the KKK.

As many of the social extremes were rising to dominance, a society of youth was emerging that was shaping many aspects and philosophies of our lives. If I was a prolific writer, I could better explain the tensions and the environment on the streets of America at this time of chaos.

The prejudice, the bigotry, the political climate, and the education system of our country, seemed to have fallen apart. A mistrust of authority began to infiltrate our youth. Prayer was removed from our schools. Mainstream religion was viewed as hypocritical and irrelevant to many. In just a few years, even abortion would become legal.

As a rebellious young man, I found myself right in the middle of all this confusion.

Now we are attending schools that are very different from what we attended in our elementary school days. It's the mid to late '60s. I am attending new schools in the heart of Clarksville. The next few years shaped me (unfortunately, in the wrong direction).

At this time we were living very close to an area that was plagued with a rough style of living. It was a notorious housing project that had a reputation for being a place where you would not want your children hanging out. It was during this time that I decided it would be a good idea to start hanging out with my newfound friends in the projects. At this time, as I saw it through the eyes of a young man, segregation wasn't enforced in the projects. Summit Heights, as the projects were called, were made up of predominantly white folks. Some of the residents were angry, mean racists.

Tough guys and gals with names like Snake, Bad Eye, and Red, weren't to be messed with. In the hallways of junior high and high school, they didn't mingle with the crowd. They were generally in a small group and usually left alone by the other students. So often, they were the ones fighting in the hallways, the bleachers of the gymnasium, and on the basketball court. They were the angry youth of the '60s. The guys with long hair and the girls with mini skirts did not have much direction. Their styles were influenced by the times.

My oldest brother, Junior, is now attending Clarksville High School. An old, two-story brick building on the corner of Greenwood Avenue and Madison Street. He wasn't really into smoking and drinking as much as some of the youth of that day but he was into fast cars, nice clothes, and girls. Even as a teenager, he understood the meaning of working to get ahead. It took money to aspire to the lifestyle that he wanted. He worked as a grill cook in a restaurant that was inside a local bowling alley where many of the youth hung out.

My brother, Kenneth, and I wanted to party. So we sought out the crowd that was notorious for smoking and drinking. This, in later years, brought about the demise of my brother Kenneth. Thankfully, drugs were not very prevalent in our circle of friends. Our preferences were beer and vodka. However, in years to come, many of them became involved in the drug scene, and it cost the lives of more than a few of my old friends — many of them died too young.

As I write today, I am nearing my 70th birthday. I am stopping to ponder things that have happened in my life. A very kind and loving mother. A father, even with all his weaknesses, still provided for his family of five boys and one girl. The boys went off the rails, but our loving sister did not go in the same direction. I think my mother must have thought, "My boys are a little out of control, but I'm going to hold tight to my sweet young daughter and shelter her." My mother gave her attention, taught her right from wrong, and prayed that she wouldn't go in the wrong direction. To this day, my only sister is one of the kindest, sweetest people I know. I now realize my mother's influence was shaping the good parts of us. As much as I loved my father, his lifestyle was influencing us in the wrong way. Ways that we would later regret.

At this time, my mother was getting very involved with a little Pentecostal church at 1470 Golf Club Lane. This was a small building that was at one time a beer joint. This building was set very close to the edge of Golf Club Lane. You could hardly park a car between this building and the road. Our family, the Mays family, and the Wilbanks family were at the first service at this little Apostolic church. There are currently seven original members still living.

My mother was becoming very faithful and was involved in the early stages of the church. She was leading the congregational singing and teaching Sunday School. That church, Apostolic Faith Tabernacle, is still there today. The founding pastor, Reverend RC Mays, and his family were working very hard and sacrificing to establish a place of refuge for the lost. My mother encouraged me to attend Sunday school. My father very seldom went, but he did go for a little while. The things I learned in that little storefront church are still with me to this day.

*I*n the future, the older boys of the family strayed from that little place of worship. My mother held on to that place of peace. A place to escape the horrors of an unfaithful husband and a home life that was emotionally draining her daily.

The bricklaying preacher that I told you about, who came into our lives in the late 50s, was still there. Still reaching, praying, preaching, still faithful. Trying to dig families out of the miry clay. But unfortunately, the church at that time wasn't for my brothers and me.

Looking back, I now realize how our lack of interest in the things of God was beginning to affect our two younger brothers, Mark and Timmy. Kids often follow in the footsteps of older siblings. Hoodlums as we were called, would romp and stomp all over the city, thinking we were bad (a phrase used for tough guys). I can distinctly remember at this time, my little brother, Timmy would hang out with us. I don't know why Timmy would do it, but he had a habit of peering into garbage cans. Looking for anything of value. It was so obvious to all of us that we nicknamed him boo boo after the little bear that followed Yogi around. (Remember?)

*I*t was getting bad for the older boys, especially Kenneth and me. The drinking and carousing around was getting way out of hand. We were now smoking every day. Bumming cigarettes from anyone that could supply them. We were skipping school and hiding all of these things from our mother and father. We thought we were hiding everything but often our parents would receive a call from the local truant officer.

I did not enjoy school at all. I would go in the front door and out the back. I went out the gym window one time at Greenwood Jr. High School. Mr. Brandon, the principal, and I became very well acquainted while I was attending Greenwood. At the end of the 9th grade at Greenwood, I know it's going to be hard to believe, but we ended up back in the country, in the same old house, on the same old gravel road.

Chapter 7

"Bad Moon Rising"

*N*ow, things are starting to get ugly. You know it's been said, "Hindsight is 20/20." I know, as adults, we often use this old phrase. If I put myself into my teen years, I would be thinking, "What in the world is that old man talking about, when he says hindsight is 20/20?" He simply means that looking back we can see more clearly than when looking into the future. Looking back we can watch the sequence of events that bring us to where we are now. An odor or a pleasant scent may arouse our memories of a certain place in time. A vision of an old house. A view of the countryside. A cul-de-sac, or a city street, may take us back to the place we grew up.

The smell of certain foods may bring me back to my mama's kitchen. The sound of a train whistle, an automobile motor, a motorcycle, birds singing, geese flying over, an airplane, and songs drifting through an old screen door. The splash of a fish in the water. These sights and sounds can sometimes take us back to better days.

We say things like, "I can remember that." We can remember when something significant in our lives happens. There is usually a trigger that takes us back to that happier time, or even to a time of hurt and sorrow. We discuss past events with our friends and loved ones and we talk about certain places and people.

I can recollect one time we were riding down the road with my parents, and my older brothers and I were misbehaving or what we called cutting up in the back seat. My father looked up in the rearview mirror and said to us, "Keep it up and I'm going to put you out and make you walk home." Sure enough, we kept it up. He pulled over to the side of the road and said, "Get out." And we got out. I can remember my mother's face, "Are you putting them out?" And he did just that. What's funny is this car was a 1963 maroon-colored Cadillac, almost brand new, with an optional bubble wrap type material on the seats to protect them. My daddy was picky about his car seats. It was a lesson in parenting that I always remembered, right or wrong. You be the judge. But, I remember he always did what he said he would do. He always taught in words and deeds that we should always keep our word.

So let me back up and go where I intended to go before I wandered down that rabbit trail of remembrance, I was speaking of how our senses bring back memories. The places we go. The smells, what we feel, tangible things, and intangible things we hold. The sights we see and what we hear prompt us and carry us to different times.

For me, what takes me back to certain times and places is music. The church hymns that my mother was leading. Even in my wildest days, these hymns were coming back to me, at times in a drunken stupor, "Just a little talk with Jesus makes it right," "I'll fly away," "Oh, I want to see him." I was working hard to shed these old songs from my memory bank by replacing them with the music of the day.

The old hangouts, especially the old bowling alley, had a jukebox right in the center of the building. Across from the jukebox, sat a pool table and the flipper machines. We fed money into them with a frenzy, always saying," I'm going to beat it this time." Fighting for the high score, a hero for a day! And by the way, the house always wins.

Now, there seems to be a competition for my soul. My mother's voice singing the old hymns was competing with that old jukebox. "B-17," "Wild Thing," "Louie, Louie," or "The Last Train to Clarksville."

By this time, the Beatles' music had almost become easy listening. Music was getting darker. Rock music was now the genre of heavy, often rebellious lyrics. Reaching into the minds of the youth who were already disenchanted with the system. Now songs like "House of the Rising Sun." And "I Can't Get No Satisfaction," seemed to be the anthems of the '60s. And in the late '60s, "Bad Moon Rising," by Creedence Clearwater Revival was climbing in the charts. A song of death and destruction.

My mother and little sister were singing hymns. My father was "Walking the Floor Over You" with Earnest Tubb. "Crazy" by Patsy Cline, "Your Cheatin' Heart" by Hank Williams, Sr., and "Hello Walls," by Willie Nelson and Marty Robbins, singing about "El Paso." And we boys were marching to a different drum.

I hate junior high, I'm walking in one end of the school and right out the other end. I'd rather be on the streets, but somehow, in the midst of all of this, I managed to make passing grades. We made it through 8th and 9th grade. My oldest brother, Junior, was getting close to graduating from Clarksville High School. But at this time, my father and mother, for financial reasons, decided to move back into the old country house once again.

I can take you to houses in the different counties that we lived in. It was not unusual for us to live in a house for only a few months. I can remember my father building a house that we would excitingly move into, only to move out very soon after we moved in. The reason for this, he would sell the new house to turn a profit. My family always held onto the property in the country, between Bellsburg and Jackson's Chapel communities.

We held on to the old home place because it technically belonged to my mother. It was part of my grandmother's place which my grandfather had taken the liberty to divide among his children. This division of land was done very randomly. For example, Betty Jane, my mother, "You take from this Holler to that Holler," and John Dee, "You take from this field to that field." AC, "This part is yours." Donald Lee, "This is for you," Bud, "This is yours." Jack Bruce, "You can have the old green bean field with the woods behind it." For the remaining girls, he left the Old Batson homeplace and the land around it. It kinda reminds me of a biblical patriarch, dividing the inheritance, without the staff and the beard.

Now we are back in the country, surrounded by aunts and uncles, our kinfolks. Grandmama and Granddaddy, again just living across the Holler. Our little innocent family has changed. Some for the better, but mostly for the worse.

I was determined that I'd had enough schooling. It was the beginning of my sophomore year at Charlotte High School in Dickson County, so I quit school. The county was not so strict in those days. I wanted to build houses. Well, not build them, but at least be a part of the framing process.

You see, just about every adult male in our part of the country was in construction. Mostly carpenters, Framing or trim carpenters. I had a great uncle, my grandfather's brother who was named Carl Batson. He was a major player in the house-building business in Nashville, Tennessee. He once told me he built more than 10,000 houses in the Metro Nashville area. So he brought many of the country bumpkins off the ridge, as it was called back then, Route One Charlotte, into his business. He taught them the building trade and paid it forward to the community he was raised in.

I loved it! I had found my calling in life. I wanted to continue to work in the trade my father had taught me so much about. You have heard the old saying, "I'd rather do that than eat." That's where I was—I could drive nails, read blueprints, use a skill saw, etc. without an education. I went to work with an all-adult, grown men framing crew. I was in Hog Heaven. I was receiving top pay. I had the tiger by the tail or so it seemed. But, look out!!! Because change was coming.

Chapter 8

A Day In The Sun

*T*he day that I did not listen to my father, I was a rebellious and very reckless teenager, just a few months shy of my 16th birthday. I thought I had the world on a rope with a downhill pull. I was physically strong for a young man. Not very big in stature. Working in the winter with an all-adult framing crew, I had built up muscle, especially in my arms and legs. I desired to be a framing carpenter. Framers as they were called or the framing crew, were usually made up of redneck white boys who loved the challenge of starting with just the foundation of a building, usually a house, and taking it to the place in the construction process where anyone could see how the structure was going to look. Homes that were so enormous people would pass by and say, "Oh look that is going to be beautiful."

The hard work was very challenging and physically demanding. Walking on top of a wall, with only a three-and-a-half-inch 2x4 under our feet. Sometimes two or three stories up in the air was something that could make a country boy proud. At the end of the day the greatest command from the boss was simply this: get up the tools, roll up the extension cords, put the ladders on the truck. Don't forget to tie them down. One more day, tired and worn out, but satisfied with the accomplishments of the day. We were always anxious to do it again the next day.

For some reason the kind of men that were in this profession not only believed in hard work they also believed in hard play. It wasn't unusual at all after a hard day's work, to stop at a local market and pick up a six-pack of beer and drink it on the way home. Not knowing or not caring that my introduction to the drinking scene would cost me dearly in the future. A price that I would pay, for the rest of my life.

Most of us who have been fortunate enough to grow older have seen seasons come and go. Cold winters, early falls, hot summers, and beautiful springs. The trees are budding and the flowers are blooming. On occasion, we have seen the year after the snow stops falling and spring comes in early. We were familiar with the days getting warm much sooner than it usually does. This was one of those years. It was the spring of '69. One of those early spring days that seem to jump right into summer. In April we were able to work with our shirts off. This was not unusual for country boy framers. We would tan from the waist up. It would almost look like we had two different bodies. If you compared the tans of our faces to the tans of our legs, it would look like two different people. Later on, this two-tone tan would be the talk of emergency room doctors and nurses.

I can remember an old country song that was about "Lonely Weekends." Roughneck, Beer-Drinking White Boys. Country-Boy Living, Honky Tonkin, Beer-Joint-Hopping, Girl-Chasing Weekends. Even at a young age, I was following the crowd. We would get paid on Friday and our pay would be gone by Monday. It was quite pitiful when I look back on those days. I was headed down a dead-end road, but God had mercy on me. He also had a plan.

Patiently sitting and waiting for friends to pick me up. Excited about the coming events of the day. With no idea that before this day was over, my life would be changed forever. A '65 Mustang pulls off the old gravel road where we lived. I was on the front porch of our old home place. I stood up and anxiously made my way to that Mustang. As we got settled in I can still remember my father walking out to the car and telling the driver, my friend Wayne, to "be careful." In the country, language like this means behave yourself and don't get into trouble. My father had a pretty good under-standing of boys who thought they were old enough to do as they pleased because he had five of them.

It was one of those almost-summertime-feeling spring days of April. It was Saturday, April 26th, 1969. We had big plans. Some of the guys with whom I hung out had made plans to go to the lake. We just wanted to see what mischief we could get into and drink a few beers. Hanging out on the shore near the water, getting there early before the crowd arrived. Whatever it was, it just didn't matter much. We were there to have fun, or so we thought.

We were packed up, packed in, and ready to go. Putting life behind us. Free as birds. Today we're going to do as we please. There were five or six of us tightly squeezed into that little Mustang but that was okay. It was time to party. The radio was blaring. There was a new song playing. Volume was turned up, "Sweet Caroline." People are still singing that song 50-plus years later. We were away from home. No parents to tell us what to do. No one to tell us that we should not be doing the things that we were doing.

We are on our way down Old Highway 79 toward Dover, Tennessee. Our driver and the owner of the Mustang looked much older than he was. I believe he was 17 or almost 18, but he could pass for someone much older. He was not old enough to buy alcohol, but he did. A little market on Dover Road had no problem filling his order. We were set now.

Passing the cans of Country Club Malt Liquor around, laughing, joking, cursing, and ready to party.

It has always been amazing to me how we have to grow old, to understand regrets. I heard someone say recently that our looks are determined by who our parents are but our lives are determined by the decisions we make. I get a little put out when I hear adults say that my life went downhill because of the way I was raised. To me, that's a cop-out. I made some poor decisions but they were my decisions.

I can remember crossing an old rusty metal bridge that went across Kentucky Lake. At Paris Landing, after you cross the bridge going west, a few hundred yards on the left is Paris Landing State Park. We had been there many times. Drinking and swimming, just looking for some excitement. As we approached the swimming area at the edge of the lake, I made one of those sudden bad decisions. This is going to sound crazy but after getting out of the car I kicked off my shoes and I began to run as fast as I could. At the same time, I was peeling off my shirt. So foolish. I don't remember removing anything from the pockets of my jeans that I had just purchased the day before. I can remember running at full speed toward the shoreline. The next thing I know I'm sailing through the air toward the water but I have a major problem. There's not much water where I'm diving.

I later learned it was between 9 and 12 inches deep. I can distinctly remember hitting bottom. I can see the mud and the sand as my face presses into the muck and mire at the bottom of the lake. I'm stunned. I can't move. I passed out for a few seconds. I don't know how but I had the fortitude to hold my breath. I must breathe but my face is buried in the bottom of the lake. I've got to breathe. I must breathe. I can't hold my breath much longer. I was almost ready to take a breath. I had held my breath as long as I possibly could.

All of a sudden I can feel myself being pulled or dragged from the lake. With silt and debris on my face, with my arms outstretched, I can remember my chest rubbing against the gravel and sand as I was pulled toward the shoreline. What's wrong with me? I'm in shock and tremendous pain.

My friends are gathered around me. I can see them now. They are distraught and confused, they're also trying to understand what's happening. I can remember looking up and seeing their faces. The confusion and terror in their eyes. I remember telling them that I would be okay. I'm just stunned. That's when I made a crucial mistake. I tried to sit up. When I attempted to raise a few inches, I felt as though a thousand sharp needles were pricking my body all over. Piercing needles of severe pain and agony. That's when I passed out for the second time.

I'm awake again. Someone is using scissors. I can sense them cutting my clothes. What are they doing to me? Why are they cutting the legs of my brand-new jeans? What's going on? What is that thing around my neck? Am I lying on a board? Where am I? I have been loaded into an ambulance. What is that loud noise? Is that a siren? Are the police chasing us? That was when I realized that I was in a vehicle, moving very fast.

Remember this was 1969. If there was a Life Flight helicopter available, it did not come for me. I later learned that the first ambulance was similar to a hearse. It stopped at the nearest hospital for an evaluation. I was then transferred to a more modern ambulance. For the next few hours, I was moving toward Vanderbilt Hospital, a place where I would spend the next 63 days of my life.

While being taken out of the ambulance, I briefly came to again. I can remember looking into the eyes of my dear mother as she witnessed her son being rolled into the emergency room. I could see the anguish on her face as my father held her up. Her legs were weak and tears were running down her cheeks.

Who is that using a drill? I know what a drill sounds like because we use them and other power tools while working on buildings. Why do I hear a drill? Someone is drilling holes in the back of my skull.

I'm feeling some pain but mostly pressure. I am so scared and confused. I've never been to this place before. A bright light is shining on my face. I can hear voices. Male and female voices barking out orders with a sense of urgency. His neck is broken. At what level? It's broken at C7. What does that mean? Now I'm finally starting to become more aware, more awake. Where am I? You're having emergency surgery at Vanderbilt Medical Center in Nashville, Tennessee.

Later that morning I would be moved to intensive care. Questions, questions. Why do I feel like I'm being pulled out of the bed head first? What is that weight that keeps pulling on my head? I don't understand. All I know is that this is the worst pain I've ever experienced. Little did I know, when I decided to be the first in the water, it would be the last time that I would ever run. According to my neurologist as he was speaking to my parents, "If he makes it for the next 24 hours, he'll never walk again."

Chapter 9

63 Days

I can't feel my legs. My toes won't move. There is something wrong with my hands. My fingers are starting to draw. Why is this happening to me? I'm young, I'm only 15 years old. I should be able to run, throw a football, or play second base on the local boys' baseball team. But now I'm stuck in a hospital bed. I find myself depending on nurses and orderlies to take care of all the personal things that I can no longer do for myself. It's frustrating. It's embarrassing. There is just no dignity. The catheter, the bedpans, the sponge baths. Will it never end?

I'm in a room with a bunch of strangers. People are coming and going. Beds are in rows, similar to pictures that I've seen of army barracks. Next to me, with some distance between us, is a gentleman lying on the strangest-looking bed I've ever seen. I'm lying on my side now and facing his bed. It's very odd because, like me, he is not supposed to stay in one position too long. The bed is circular. If you can imagine a large open wheel, with a bed laying across it, and when the wheels turn, the man on the bed is either facing the floor or facing the ceiling. Ever so often, the nurses or orderlies would come into the room and flip him over. I learned that this procedure was to help prevent bedsores from lying in one position too long. This had to be performed for him as he remained in traction. He had one hook screwed into his skull and a weight hanging from that hook. It was a dreadful sight for a 15-year-old who hadn't fully comprehended what was happening to himself, much less being in a ward of spinal injury patients.

I'll never forget the pain, I can't even describe it. It's not just physical, it's emotional. After approximately ten days, the traffic of those coming to see their friend began to subside. They witnessed the celebrity, the tough guy who is no longer tough. All the jokes and laughter that they have tried to use to cheer me up. Those smiles have now turned to pity as my fair-weather friends become less frequent visitors.

I began to realize who cared for me. As I look back and realize the sacrifices my mother and father were making to try to navigate the difficulties that my injury had brought upon their everyday lives. The worry, the heartache, the financial burden that has suddenly been thrust upon them. My mother would come often, at times almost every day. As I look back and think about the sacrifices that she had made to be by my side, it was tremendous.

As I mentioned earlier, at the beginning—our family would mostly be categorized as poor. We lived from week to week. Never anything extra. We were a one-vehicle family most of the time and my father would need that vehicle to get back and forth to work. Looking back, I don't know how my mother could have been so faithful to be by my side unless neighbors and loved ones helped her to get to the hospital regularly. At least this was the case for the first couple of weeks. I can remember telling my mother, "Momma, you don't have to be here every day." I believe it hurt her feelings, and I have always regretted it. But I believed it was for the best, for her and the family. Remember, there were still five kids at home. Two were old enough to pretty much take care of themselves. But at this time, three were under the age of 12.

Tonight, the nurses and doctors are scrambling. They have called my parents. Something is wrong with me. I'm burning up. What is that smell? It's the smell of rubbing alcohol. I am delirious. I'm coming and going. I'm in more pain than ever. Gentlemen in white coats are gathered at my bedside. Not just on one side of the bed, but on both sides. I can hear them speaking. We must get his fever down. I'm having delusions. Why am I stuck between two-floor joists? Somebody help me. I can't get out. The joists are pressing against both of my upper arms and shoulders. I can't breathe. And now they tell me the next day, "You were almost gone."

Now I find myself, and I'm ashamed to admit it, bitter, angry, disgusted, just wanting to die. Yes, it got that bad. I'm getting tired of the probing and the poking, the needles, the IV tubes, the traction, and the constant pressure on my head and neck. The pain, the medication that did not seem to stop the pain anymore. The breathing treatments were a daily chore. And I do mean a chore. "Breathe in, breathe out." "Use your diaphragm." "You've got to learn all over again how to breathe properly." **Lady**, **Nurse**, you are mean, too mean. Why do you keep on pushing me to do something so hard? And by the way, that physical therapist is doing the same thing. I can still hear her saying, "You've got to move your joints, stretch your muscles." "It's going to help you stay limber." "You cannot afford to stiffen up." She had no mercy on me. She made me cry.

Days turned into weeks. Routines became almost monotonous. I'm learning how to hold a fork. Such a simple task that we take for granted until we can't do it. The neurologist is seeing me quite often. I'll never forget his kindness. His name was Doctor Arthur Gernt Bond. He would come into my room and almost every time he would use a little device that resembled an ink pen with a little pointed wheel on the end. He would roll that little device on my feet and legs, always asking, "Can you feel that?" he would say. "What about that?" He would reach behind my neck and press his finger into my spine, never saying much, just writing on a chart that was in a tray at the end of my bed until the next time. Pretty much the same every day. I still could not move anything from my chest down. With very limited use of my arms and hands.

I know what I'm going to say may not even seem believable, but at the time, 1969, Vanderbilt Hospital was not the ultra-modern facility that we see today. Most of the hospital was very old, with a '40s or '50s vibe. Tile floors, painted walls, and wards with several beds in each ward. All wooden windows had to be raised by the staff to get some air flowing. Crank-up beds. I don't even remember the rooms having TVs. My only entertainment was a small, portable radio that a physical therapist brought me. I love physical therapists! Even though at the time, the hospital, by today's standards, was dated, Vanderbilt was still considered one of the best hospitals in America, especially for traumatic injuries. I was very blessed to be there.

On this day, something miraculous happened to me. I had somewhat gotten accustomed to the monotony of everyday hospital living. It's now the morning of the 57th day that I have been here. The morning starts like many others, same old, same old. From the time of my stay up until this point, I have been fortunate enough to have visitors. However, sometimes even further between visits, there were that faithful few who week in and week out still came to see me. One particular man, a preacher, a pastor, by the name of RC

Mays, would visit, and he would pray before he left my room. This day was pretty much the same, except for one major difference. This day, he prayed, and God heard the prayer. A few minutes later he left the room. After that, I began to move my toes. After I realized my toes were moving, I began to scream, "Nurse, nurse!" A nurse came into my room. When she realized what was happening, she began to run down the hall towards the nurse's station, telling everyone she met what had just happened. She called my neurologist to deliver the good news. In just a few minutes Dr. Bond came into the room and he was very happy. There was hope!

If you are reading this and you don't believe in miracles that is certainly your prerogative but remember I was the one lying there for 57 days without moving. Now, I believe that God performed a miracle for me that day.

With some help, using two canes, I was able to walk from a wheelchair to get into my parent's car six days later. For a total of 63 days, and the miracle that had changed my life. While we were loading up the car, my mother went to the business office to make payment arrangements. When she got to the office they told her that my bill had already been taken care of. We to this day have no idea who paid that bill. Our second miracle that day was the beginning of my redemption because of an accident.

I rode along in the car with my parents, looking at all the nature. The trees, the flowers, the sound of the cars as they were passing by, hearing the birds singing their melodies. Things that I hadn't been able to see or experience in 63 long days.

I had no idea what I should expect that day riding down Hwy 41A, heading home to Bellsburg. What was my life going to be like? How would the other siblings react to me? Would I ever be able to walk again? Would any of my friends ever return? Would I ever be able to work a job again? Would I ever get married and have a family? Would things ever be normal?

So many questions and so few answers!

Chapter 10

Back on My Feet

*I*t's late summer, 1969 and very hot. I can remember the hot, humid weather. My hospital bed had been put right in the middle of the living room in that old country house. Every summer, it was always a ritual to move the old warm morning wood-burning stove out of the way for the summer.

Everyone was walking past my bed to go into different parts of the old house. By this time it is a five-room house with a bath. Something happened this sultry hot summer that we had never seen before. My father came into the house with a very special gift. A gift that would relieve us from much misery. That gift was a portable, in-the-wall, air conditioner. It was a glorious day. The electrician was there. My father was cutting a hole in the wall of the living room. There was no electrical outlet at the place where the hole was being cut. It would not be very long until we had something in that old house that we never had before. Cool, refreshing air in the summertime.

Country folks called guests, visitors, kinfolks, or company were coming in and out of our house. The house was sometimes full of folks. My aunt, Marjorie, and Uncle Harold and kids, my Uncle James, my Uncle Billy, and their families. They were coffee drinkers and smokers. I can remember my Uncle JB flipping his cigarette ashes in the cuff of his pants. My mamma did not tolerate much smoking in the house.

Most smoke breaks happened outside the house, on the front or back porch.

It was kind of a crazy situation. The sleeping arrangements for our guests were very limited. As the summer began to slowly pass, the novelty of visiting and supporting the young man who had a terrible accident had subsided. Now it has become a dreaded routine that normally included my mother's determination to care for her injured son. It was bathing, dressing, and feeding. It was really hard on my family, especially my mother.

After several weeks, I began to do more for myself with a wheelchair that had been donated. With the help of a couple of canes, I could maneuver around the house. I have now begun to walk more. I would go outside and sit on the old front porch. Listen to the birds sing, and watch the dogs play. My spirit was lifted. I was determined to not let this make an invalid out of me.

My hands and legs did not work right. I had lost control of my bladder without warning. My spinal injury had messed me up, both physically and emotionally. Fortunately, as time went on, the bladder issue wasn't as debilitating. I learned to prepare and live with it. I was still in a spirit of depression. I wondered if I would ever be able to live a normal life. The fear of the unknown is what scared me the worst. I had no idea what my future would hold.

My days that summer were long and hard. I was struggling to find my new normal. Things begin to register with me, one thing in particular: I am now a cripple, physically handicapped. I challenged myself every day to adjust to my new lifestyle. I felt so alone. Those old friends hardly ever come around anymore. The motorcycle that my brother Kenneth and I shared that was given to us by our uncle Billy,

I could no longer ride. The old 1954 Chevrolet station wagon that I owned when I had my accident, I could no longer drive. My old boss called the house one day and asked "Is the old station wagon for sale?" I said yes, and sold it to him for $75. I can still remember him coming to our house, and driving it away, up the old gravel road. I hated to see it go.

When I left the hospital in late June, my neurologist came into my room to dismiss me. I can only remember one thing that he said. I remember him getting very serious and telling me, "The best therapy that you can do is to always keep moving. Don't lay dormant. Get up every day and move. You may not be able to do everything you once did, but you will be able to do something."

In my life, I have thought about this one piece of advice more than a 1,000 times. I did not know at the time that my life would hold some very low moments. Many times in the future I would revert to this simple advice, and remind myself to get up and keep moving.

This is going to sound a little crazy, but my goal every day for several weeks was to walk from our front porch out to an old garage in front of the house. Looking back on this daily challenge or therapy that was so hard at the time, I now realize that the distance between the porch and the garage wasn't more than 75 feet. But, it was the longest 75 feet for me. I would walk to the garage and rest, and then walk back to the front porch.

My father had built the garage many years ago, sometime in the fifties. It was a pole structure with a tin roof. On the sides were vertical sawmill planks of different widths that were weathered to a gray color. No garage door, it just opened in the front. To my knowledge, it was never used much for a garage, mostly for junk. My father was odd in some ways. He did not like a messy yard. Although the yard had very little grass and was not very pretty, my father wanted us to keep the junk in that old garage. On the very back wall, I can remember an old workbench that was always covered with a scattering of assorted tools. A few mechanics tools, a socket wrench, an assortment of sockets, wrenches, pliers, etc…

My uncle Jackie has brought an old Corvair over to our house to work on. If you are familiar with this model of Chevy, it was a small car with an engine in the rear. The Corvair had several issues as I recall. The main issue was it would not run. The night my Uncle Jackie pulled it to our house and parked it in front of the garage inspired me. His goal was to find a good motor and replace the one that would not run. But I had a brainstorm. I could help him. So with a few wrenches and sockets, I started taking that old Corvair apart. It was never repaired but it was excellent therapy.

I'm 16 years old now, summer is almost over, and school is getting ready to start for the year, I need to go back to school because I will need an education. These were the thoughts of my parents more than my thoughts. They were thinking about my future, and in all honesty, even more than I was. I did not relish the idea of going back to school. I had dropped out before my accident and I did not want to go back. My mother insisted, so we went to Charlotte High to enroll me in high school. I had finished the 9th grade before dropping out, but to our surprise, the principal of Charlotte High told my mother they were not equipped to handle a handicapped student.

Remember this was 1969. Handicapped accessibility was not a norm in buildings at that time. So the powers to be recommended a trade school in Nashville which was pretty much out of the question. Now what in the world am I going to do? This was a big question. Was I going to be a burden to my family for the rest of my life, living on government subsidies and programs for the crippled?

What happens next is one of the greatest opportunities that has ever been given to me. My Uncle Bud came to see me. We were always pretty close before my accident. One summer he gave me one of my first, sure enough, legitimate jobs. I would help him frame houses; he, like most of the men on the ridge, was a carpenter. Now, he was going to do something different. He is going to work for my great Uncle Bruce in his newly established hardware and building supply store.

Midway Supply Company on Cumberland Street in Ashland City, Tennessee, was sitting next to the old railroad. Everything to build a house except Ready Mix Concrete, this was my Uncle Bruce's motto. My Uncle Bud said to me "I'm going to work for Uncle Bruce and I want you to go with me."

I was walking better by now but I had this hip and leg-swinging gait. My knees would not bend very much; I had to shuffle my legs, using my hips to walk. My uncle was always positive that they would find plenty of things that I could do.

My first job every morning was to sprinkle floor sweep on the sealed concrete floor and then sweep with a wide push broom. I was very good at my first job. Before long I was stocking shelves. Learning about profit margins, taking inventory, and working with some old experienced hardware guys that my Uncle Bruce had hired. I was acquiring knowledge that I would never have learned in school.

I became one of my uncle's main buyers for the hardware part of the store. Back then it was done the old-fashioned way. Hardware salesmen would come around usually one time a week and you would purchase what was needed for another week, usually in small batches of multiple items. It was while working in the public that I began to realize that many people I came in contact with were kind, but I could see on their faces and in their eyes, the look of pity. Children would often ask their parents, "What is wrong with that man, why does he walk that way?" Occasionally I would fall, but after a while, I learned to just get up and shake it off. It was during this time that I learned to somewhat overcome the stigma of my condition.

At approximately 17 years old I started getting serious about living for God. I had started going to church as much as possible at an Apostolic Church in Clarksville. Pastored by Reverend RC Mays, I attended Sunday school at this church as a child. During my time in Vanderbilt Hospital, Reverend Mays had come to see me many times. He was very consistent and persistent. I had told him several times that if the Lord would let me walk again, I would give my life to Him.

I had made a promise and I intended to keep that promise. After many times of going to the altar, I decided it was time for the next step, Baptism. In the basement of the church, there was a beautiful rock baptismal pool that Reverend Mays had built with his own hands. The water would cascade down from the top of the rocks into a rock reservoir. This was the place where in the future, many of my family and friends would have their sins washed away, and in years to come, my children would be baptized in that old baptistry.

I fell in love with God. What was at first a promise to serve God, now had blossomed into a relationship between myself and the Lord. At 17 years old, I received the baptism of the Holy Ghost and with the spirit of God within me, I now had a brand new life. I had been born again.

I've always had a love for music. My tastes varied from Rock, Motown, Country, Pop, etc. After I started going to church I fell in love with many of the old hymns, "Amazing Grace," "When We All Get to Heaven," "Unseen Hand," and "Just A Little Talk with Jesus," just to name a few. Pastor Mays' children were very talented. He had two boys and two girls. They sang many songs that the southern gospel groups of that day sang.

We began to go to the concerts that were held at the War Memorial Auditorium in Nashville. These all-night singings, as they were called, were very thrilling. We saw live and in person some of the greats: JD Summer and the Stamps, The Happy Goodmans, The Oak Ridge Boys, The Dixie Echoes, The Downings, The Rambos, and too many to name. They put something in me that made me want to sing. For a while, I did sing with several church groups, but God had other plans for me.

Chapter 11

Blue Eyed- Dark-Haired- Irish Girl

I 'm dedicating this chapter to my wife of 51 years. Irish is more prevalent on my father-in-law's side of the family. The red hair, freckles, and light skin were from his side. My mother-in-law was a beautiful dark-haired woman with raven black hair. The hair color was from her Cherokee heritage. With this union, my wife was given her mother's beauty and her father's Irish determination and willingness to work and succeed.

God knew what I needed, so he gave me a beautiful and strong wife both emotionally and physically. You've heard it said about some people, that they don't have a lazy bone in their body, and it's a true thing about my wife—Diane Wilbanks Reynolds. My wife's hard-working father had a saying that went something like this "If I don't have anything to do, I'm still going to get up every day and do it."

On September 15th, 1972, I became a married man and Sandra Diane became a married woman. It was not a whirlwind romance of just a few weeks, we had known each other since we were 7 years old. She was 18 and I was 19 years old, starting our lives together in a rented house for $65 a month and a job making less than $100 a week. Ten-and-a-half months later our first child was born. A baby girl named after me, Ricki Michelle Reynolds. Boy could she cry. This was just the beginning, two more children would follow, all girls.

Looking back, to be in the physical condition I was in, I still had a real determination to succeed. I wanted to be a good husband, a good father, and a good Christian. I know at times I failed at all of these things. I had decided to ask my Uncle Bruce for a raise. I had a family and we needed more money. To describe my Uncle Bruce as a hard-nosed businessman would have been an understatement. He pretty much played by his own set of rules. I needed more money but he was not giving in.

I thought to myself "I'm going to open up my own store with a business partner." So my wife and I, and my business partner and his wife opened up a paint and floor covering store in Ashland City. We successfully ran Ri-Don's Decorating Center for five years with a partner and then for eight more years we operated it on our own. I eventually sold the business and went to work selling building supplies.

During these 13 years, our other two children came along. We did not necessarily plan for them, life happened. Our middle daughter, Crystal Dian Reynolds—A dark-haired blue-eyed beauty, who favored both of us. This middle child of ours already had a mind of her own. She had much determination and lots of personality. She was the apple of her Papa's eye. He thought she had hung the moon. My father-in-law dipped snuff. One day as he was holding Crystal's hand and walking across the road, to get her something from the store I'm sure, he spat and the wind caught it and Crystal angrily told him, "YOU PIT IN MY EYE."

Our youngest with light hair and bright blue eyes, Misty Dawn Reynolds, is a beauty but for the first few months a little bit weak. She became very ill while I was at work one day. My wife called and said come quickly to the hospital. The doctors were very concerned. I remember getting the call but I did not rush straight to the hospital. I stopped at home for a little while. I know some may be reading this and saying to yourself, is this man an idiot? The reason I stopped at home for a few minutes was to go into my child's room, kneel beside the bed, and ask God for his healing power. You know what, it worked—she now has four beautiful children of her own. GOD IS STILL A MIRACLE WORKER!!! LOOK WHAT HE HAS GIVEN US.

Chapter 12

All In

I have never been able to understand or comprehend how a father or a mother could walk away from their children. My mother and father showed me by example that we were in it for the long haul. I know that some of our parenting skills were acquired from watching the actions of our parents. We have children. We bring these innocent humans into this world, with very little knowledge about what we are doing. Not even an understanding of the awesome responsibility that we have taken on. As I try to describe the magnitude of importance that parenting brings to us, I also must emphasize that most young parents have no clue. We did not get a practice run. We learned something new every day.

The joy can be overwhelming but the panic can also send us as parents into an oblivious state. It can shock us with the realization of how little we know. My wife and I were raised in a generation with a philosophy that we heard many times from the older generation. It was a very simple quote from the old folks, here it is, "You made your bed now you have to sleep in it." They would say it in many different ways. Stop whining, don't expect someone to raise your children for you. They are yours to raise. Figure it out. We'll help you but we're not doing it for you.

When babies are crying they're either wet or hungry or maybe cold or hot. Nobody said it would be easy. I know some of this sounds harsh but I knew our children belonged to us. They did not belong to their grandparents.

In this chapter of our lives, as parents in our twenties, we found ourselves as lost as a goose in a hail storm. Most days we struggled to raise our three daughters who were different but also they were so much alike.

I would like to insert something here that I have thought about many times. It may sound odd to you but I have noticed something. When a medical doctor, a dentist, a lawyer, or other professionals apply their trade, even after many years of preparation and education, they often use the phrase that they are practicing.

So I believe it is fair to say that most parents spend a lot of time practicing. We did not have trial runs. Everything seemed to be learned as we progressed. Our happy-go-lucky lives are thrown into a tailspin of struggles and trials. Lots of heartaches and joy at the same time. We are growing up but we don't realize it at the time. Our patience is being stretched to the limit. Our love for our spouse, children, and our family are taking root.

The advice we receive, good or bad, begins to help make us into the people that we are going to become. We begin to realize that the older we get, the smarter our parents become. The memories that our children have of us and the early years of their lives will be forever embedded into their personalities and attitudes. My wife and I found ourselves with three lovely daughters and their very livelihood would depend on our faithfulness and devotion for their well-being.

I am struggling physically. My legs don't work right. I have limited use of my hands. I have a wife and three children but for some silly reason that I cannot fully explain, I never believed that there was anything that I could not do.

My wife was more than just a pretty face. Never complained about her motherly responsibilities. Our three girls meant everything to her. I have no doubt she would lay down her life if she had to save one of our children. The greatest thing that we have going for us, other than determination and persistence, is the fact that we put our trust in God. We've always believed that He was Faithful and True.

By this time in our lives, our little family had become very active in an Apostolic Church in Clarksville. The church had opened up a Christian School. My wife became very involved in the school and worked faithfully in it. Our goal and determination to educate our children in a Christian environment was not just a preference, it was a conviction. Our three girls graduated from Apostolic Christian School, went to college, and have become quite successful.

For the next several years there would be many tears, heartaches, and sacrifices made to accomplish the goals that we had set for ourselves. We spent many days and nights laughing through our tears, the greatest of human emotions. We raised our girls in the admonition of the Lord. Of this, we have no regrets.

Chapter 13

Good Times Or Bad Times Don't Last Forever

*A*s you know by now we were very involved in our local church. We lived in a house that joined church property. In those days everything centered around the church. It was very common to attend church 3 to 4 times a week. A revival could last for several weeks. I'm thankful for the faithful saints of God who instructed, encouraged, and loved our little family.

Our pastor and his wife had been at the church for more than 25 years at this time. He pastored for more than 40 years until his health began to fail him. While he was pastoring, he worked with vigor and determination to help people as he called it, to live right.

Our church was part of an Apostolic/Pentecostal movement that was very conservative. I know now as a Pentecostal how it may look to this modern generation. The doctrine that we grew up with would look unbelievable to them. Some today would call us old-time Holiness Pentecostals but it was a way of life for us. Being involved in what was known as worldly entertainment was out of the question. Many forms of entertainment were strictly forbidden.

We raised our girls with no TV in the house. They listened to Christian programs on the radio and did a whole lot of reading. I can remember my wife loading me down with library books to be taken to the dropbox at the library. Our girls were avid readers. So much centered around the Christian School, Bus Ministry, Church Camp Meetings, Youth

Camps, Youth Retreats, Sunday School, Choir, Preaching, Praying, Singing, and Shouting. All of this was not just part of what we did but who we were. The congregation was not large as far as numbers but a very sincere bunch of folks who genuinely loved God.

As we all know life is not always a bed of roses. People get older. Sickness overcomes. Tragedy strikes. So many times heartache hits close to home. Saints of God who have helped us along the way are called to their Eternal reward. Loved ones, grandparents, parents, even siblings are taken from us. Many times suddenly without warning. During these years of happiness there was also much sorrow. My wife lost two brothers at the age of 35 years old. Her father died suddenly of a heart attack. Her mother who lived next to us died one afternoon. It was our pastor's birthday and the church was giving him a party. My wife went over to take her mother some food before the party and found her in the bathroom, passed away.

My grandfather, whom I loved dearly, had passed away. A generation was leaving here. Stop! Why do things keep changing? The comfort and security of those we looked up to, who we put our trust in, they were leaving. How can we go on? How can we move forward? How can we go beyond this? We would find ourselves Standing on the Promises of God our Savior. I wish that I could say I'm perfect but sadly that's not possible.

Sometimes I would question the rules and regulations of the church. Why do we do this or that? Why does someone believe that this is so wrong? Who said so? All of a sudden the rebellion against the establishment rises within me. Many would say I'm not living this way. I'm tired of going to church. I'm sick of obeying the rules. Some of these doubts may have even crossed my mind but I am so thankful that His grace kept calling me back to that Old Rugged Cross where I was changed. I can say something got a hold of me. I mean something got a real hold on me. It wasn't a *think-so* or *guess-so*, it was a real *know-so* Salvation that I could feel.

I would be a liar if I told you that I have never slipped up or made mistakes. I have made many mistakes but I can honestly tell you I have never wanted to go back to the life that I lived before.

My calling to the ministry was real and very important to me. It did not start as a Pulpit Ministry. My pastor was what some would call, old school. He was kind of like this, "So you think God called you to preach that's great! Here's a broom or a vacuum cleaner. By the way, there's a toilet clogged up in the restroom." "But Pastor I'm feeling my calling." "Okay, We'll see." Some of you reading this may be thinking that he wasn't very supportive of my newfound calling, but I knew that he was happy, that someone he had helped to pull out of the miry clay was heeding God's call.

By the way, we had a whole church full of folks that he won over to God. He taught that being a soul winner was far more important than being a preacher. It's all about the souls of men and women and the children. "You want to preach! Here's a Sunday school class for you. You can teach 11 and 12-year-olds." For several years to come I taught Sunday School. Quite often I will shake hands with people who now have grandchildren, whom I was privileged to teach in a Sunday school class.

Looking back, I think quite often of the different positions that my wise old pastor placed me in. Positions like Sunday School Superintendent, Song Leader, Bible Teacher, Director of the Bus Ministry and Believe It or Not, Drummer, Sound Man, Peanut Brittle salesperson, and Associate Pastor. He was preparing me for a task that I never dreamed about. One day I would fill his position, but never his shoes.

60

Chapter 14

A Brand New House; A Brand New Job

I t's now 1988. It's the year that a book was released titled "88 Reasons Why the Lord Could Come in 88." That's right—a number-one bestseller, but you guessed it, it did not happen the way he said it would.

We're still here. I'm struggling. Trying to make a living, running a floor covering/paint store in the little town of Ashland City, Tennessee. The economy was not good and I was deep in debt. I had moved the store into a brand new strip mall. It was a much better location with good parking and lots of traffic. I was hoping to generate more business with this new move.

Not only was I moving a store, we were in the process of building a brand new house in the little community of Henrietta, Tennessee. It was looking more and more as the old saying goes that I had "bit off more than I could chew." So what do we do as Christians when we get in a jam of our own making? We ask God to get us out of it. But I had something going for me. My wife and I had always believed in giving. We believed in paying our tithes. We had always had the attitude that 10% of our income belonged to God. Something that we still practice and believe to this day.

Lord, I need some help. My help comes from the Lord. It was on a Monday morning when help came my way. A man walked in the front of my store. He walked past the showroom, the carpet displays, wallpaper books, and shelves of paint. He made his way to my office. I saw him coming as he approached my office door. Without much ado, he point-blank asked if I would be interested in selling our little floor-covering business. It was a total surprise. I had been praying but this kind of knocked me off my feet. I was thinking and kind of stammering trying to fully comprehend what was happening. I wanted out but I'm trying to contain myself. His next question was "How much?" I told him if he would come back in the morning I would price it for him. My head was spinning.

*T*he next morning I opened at my regular hour, 7:00 a.m. Just a few minutes later he came in. We greeted each other and got right down to business. He said to me "Have you come up with a price?" I said, "I have" and I quoted it to him. Without another word, he said "I'll take it. When can we close?" I said, "Give me seven days and it's yours." At the end of seven days, I was out of the floor covering business.

The Miracles did not stop there. The very week that we closed on the store, I was offered a job in sales making more than I had ever made in the floor covering business. So for the next thirteen years, I sold building supplies. We lived in a new house with our girls growing up and my wife teaching at our Christian school. By this time we now had teenagers. Please pray for us.

Chapter 15

Fate

Henrietta, Tennessee. It was just a wide spot in the road. If you drive through and blink, you might miss it. No red lights, no police force. There are a few businesses. A grocery store, a feed and farm store, a volunteer fire department, a hair salon, and a small hole-in-the-wall with a sign that reads, Mac's Dairy Shack. It's a small community of farmers and construction workers that are mostly connected to the pipeline business. It seems as though every male-abled body occupant could operate tractors, bulldozers, backhoes, and anything else with wheels.

Mac's Dairy Shack was a gathering place for many of the men. I'll only use first names here to protect the innocent. A very tall man enters the establishment. He's not very friendly. You would have to knock him down for him to speak to you. His name was Tommy. He may appear to be just another farmer but he was a Senator in the Tennessee State House of Representatives. The crowd was just about the same every day. Tommy's brother would also come in. His demeanor was even worse than his older brother's. Some would say stuck up, with a better-than-everybody-else attitude. At least those were the first impressions but when you got to know them better, you find out that it's just the way they act. It's not personal, it's just the way they were.

On several occasions, I've taken time to eat a meal or drink a cup of coffee with what I would call "the Liars Club." It was always amazing to me how these grown men would sit there, sometimes for 2 or 3 hours in the morning, and swap yarns about weather conditions, politics, and even religion. The old guys would talk about what they used to do. Someone would always say "That is not the way we did it. I'm not doing it that way." Now some young man would pop in and say "We found a better way."

*H*ave you ever been in the company of someone who just knows everything? Intelligence seems to be oozing out of their ears. Their head is larger because their brain is bigger. He's the smartest guy in the room. He's the self-proclaimed mayor of Henrietta. He technically has no authority but everything that went on in the little community, he thought he had to know about.

First impressions are not always correct. As I began to get acquainted with these good country folks at Henrietta, I realized that this was the place where we wanted to raise our daughters. We had moved from a rental house in Clarksville to a new home that we had built in Henrietta. A small, unincorporated community, on Highway 12 between Clarksville and Ashland City, Tennessee.

Let me pause here and tell you a story. Events in our lives are often determined by one or two individuals. An event that happened in the late '50s changed the course of my wife's family. I mentioned my wife's father and mother briefly at the beginning of this writing. My wife's father, who I knew as Mr. Joe or Mr. Wilbanks, was a very quiet, no-nonsense type of man. He grew up in the cotton fields of northern Mississippi and Southern West Tennessee around the community of Shiloh, Michie, and Selmer Tennessee. He was a very hard worker who believed in a day's work for a day's pay. He was a sharecropper and to my knowledge, he had no property of his own. He was always looking for ways to make things easier for his large family.

Do you remember how I said one decision can change the course of our history? Well, this happened to Mr. Wilbanks and his family. Mr. Wilbanks somehow, somewhere, acquired a magazine. I don't think anyone knows exactly what publication he was reading but it was some sort of farm journal put out most likely by a company that was catering to the farmers. The Farm Bureau even today still puts out a similar publication. In this particular magazine, the ad read something like this, *looking for a hard-working farm manager to work on a large farm in Tennessee, contact Richard Head.*

My wife's father and my soon-to-be father-in-law answered that ad and moved his family to Clarksville. Mr. Head, whom I later became acquainted with, was quite a character. A hard man to approach or at least it seemed that way to me. A tall man, quite reserved, did not talk much, at times he could be gruff. Never a lot of small talk. A man who ruled his farming kingdom with an iron fist. You could look in any direction around the community of Oak Plains and Henrietta and see his farm holdings: Cattle, Corn, Tobacco, Soybeans, and Construction. He had a hand in it all.

In the late '80s and mid-'90s, I found myself dealing with this hard-nosed businessman. I had purchased four building lots from him without more than two dozen words between us. I'm telling you the truth. Those lots were on a street called Hazel Drive, named after Mr. Head's wife. We built four houses in Hazel Estates. We lived in three of them for approximately 12 years. We sold one house to a friend and his wife. Believe it or not, I taught him in Sunday School. If it had not been for that farm journal ad and the decision that my wife's father made I would never have met her, our children would not have been born, and we would not be living in Henrietta, home of Pat Head Summitt, UT Knoxville.

Chapter 16

Our Girls

I t is the fall of 1991. We have just finished and moved into the last house that would be our home in Henrietta, Tennessee. It was not a big house, only 1200 ft. Three bedrooms, two full baths but it was large enough for our family of five.

Our two oldest daughters are getting to the age, you know, that courting age. They were showing interest in the boys or maybe I should say, young men. We now have children that are no longer kids. It's time for driver's licenses, cars, jobs, graduations, and all those activities that hold the attention of parents and teenagers.

My job as a road salesman at a building supply company kept me super busy. I had customers in five counties including the Metro Nashville area. Constant traveling from one job site to another, calling on building contractors who were regular customers, and trying to establish new contacts for future business. It was 12-hour days most days through the week. The irony is that it's the same company that my Uncle Bruce started in 1969. The company is now owned by a father and his two sons. It is a large company with multiple interests and locations. It's funny how I came full circle back to where I started as a teen. I did not have to apply for the job. The owner called me and made me an offer. I took the offer and it turned out to be the best job decision I've ever made, at least in the secular sense.

I was called because of my building supply knowledge. As I have mentioned, my family was a family of builders on my father's side and my mother's side. I had my father, brothers, uncles, cousins, nephews, and many friends who were builders of all sorts. I would call on them and they would buy from me. Maybe out of pity, but I like to think it was out of Love. I guess for different reasons but whatever the reason was okay with me. I was making a good living.

My success was coming with a price. I was seeing very little of my children. They were at a critical age. A time that I can look back on and now realize how spending time with them could have nurtured a fatherly relationship with them. A relationship that we so desperately needed.

*M*y wife and I were so busy trying to be good leaders in the church that we did not realize that our children were drifting away from us. For my part, I have regretted this lack of insight. Our girls were growing up and I did not even know them. They knew me because I stood at the head of the class or behind a pulpit. Singing in a group or a choir. Their daddy the Leader, the Singer, the Preacher, and the Provider was not reaching for his own. In the years to come, our girls seemed to struggle to find happiness with a companion. I believe sometimes they were looking for what they wanted their father to be, emotionally there for them. As young adults our three daughters had to learn some lessons the hard way.

I don't suppose there's a parent on earth that supports every decision made by their children. I don't know about every father, but I did not believe that any man was good enough for my daughters. To make that statement now sort of sounds ridiculous. It is not our place, as parents, to choose our children's husbands or wives. We hope all relationships are good but if not we'll be here, always to love and support you. Mr. Tom Bodett had a very popular commercial. A commercial promoting Motel 6. At the end, he would always say to his listening audience "We'll leave the light on for you." As parents, we should have the welcome mat out at all times.

I would like to go ahead and insert some information concerning our three daughters who we are very proud of. Our oldest daughter, Michelle, looks and acts like my mother. We sit with her every Sunday at church. She has two sons: Carson, who is married to Ashlin and will be having our great-grandson in October. Brian is working maintenance for an apartment complex here in Clarksville. Brian had the misfortune of losing his son and our great-grandson, Eli. Both sons are devoted to their mother. Good young men who would do anything for their grandparents.

Our middle daughter, Crystal, is the one so much like her father. Dark-haired, blue-eyed beauty, like her mother. Somewhat rebellious as a teen but determined to accomplish her goals. Working hard as a single mother. Putting herself through nursing school, while working to support her young son. Our first grandchild, Joseph Michael (Joey) whom his granny, Diane, absolutely adored. Joey was with his granny often as Crystal finished her nursing degree. Joey is now 28 years old. He's an air traffic controller in Minnesota. Crystal also has a daughter whose name is Kennedy. A young lady with the looks of a movie star and very smart. We were privileged to attend her college graduation at UT Chattanooga. She is now teaching high school English in Chattanooga. Crystal's husband, Matt, Kennedy's father, is a fine man. A man's man. Retired Special Forces who now flies a Life Flight helicopter out of Nashville, Tennessee. Still serving the people.

Misti, our youngest, and her husband Jeremy live about a mile from us. Misti works for the school system and Jeremy is a hydraulic mechanic. They have four children: Vada, the youngest. Very smart and very beautiful. Andrew, a 16-year-old genius who recently graduated from Clarksville High School with a full academic scholarship to the University of Tennessee, Knoxville. Bailey is smart, witty, and beautiful. She has graduated high school and has been working on her teacher's degree. She will graduate college in August and will be teaching this fall, at Liberty Elementary. Tyler, the fourth child, is not a child anymore. Tyler is in the Air Force, stationed in Georgia, married to his new bride, Britton. We love and appreciate our daughters, their husbands, and our grandchildren. We could not be more proud of them.

Chapter 17

A New Season

*H*as God ever worked on you? As I write the beginning sentence of this chapter, I pause and think, will anyone understand this question? Maybe I should rephrase the question. Has the Lord ever begun to deal with your heart, your mind, your spirit? We know enough about how the Lord sometimes communicates with his people, to realize and say to ourselves, God is trying to show me something. The Spirit is trying to get my attention.

I am now 47 years old. My wife and I are empty nesters or soon will be. I'm making a better living than ever. Two cars in the driveway. A new home, almost paid for. My wife, Diane, after 20 years of volunteer service to the Christian School, has chosen to take time off from teaching. I'm still working long hours and still really busy but something is happening to me. My dream job is losing its appeal. I'm very confused. The money is still there. Business is still good, but I am burned out. Looking back and thinking of this time in our lives, I can pinpoint the episodes that were bringing Winds of Change.

Many can remember the year 1999. The reason is that it was the year that many so-called tech experts predicted a major computer crash. When the year 2000 rolled around, your financial information would be lost. Computer systems all over the world would fail. The Mark of the Beast, Armageddon, World War III, you name it, fear was all around. The news media kept us all on edge.

$\mathcal{M}$y boss in the building supply store I was working for was a computer programmer, before stepping up to run the business. When the employees would approach the subject with fear and skepticism, he would just smile and say nothing is going to disrupt our system. Everything is being prepared. So 2000 came around with no major glitches. Around the world we were safe. Our information is still there. Money is still circulating. We are now looking forward to the new millennial.

I was stepping into the new world wrestling with decisions. A miserable man trying to find the will of God. At this time I've been in the ministry for approximately 30 years. Sitting under one Pastor, Mentor, Bishop, and spiritual father. All of the titles or positions that he held were earned by devotion, hard work, and dedication. This great man that I have looked up to and worked beside for many years, is starting to change. Subtle changes that are hardly noticeable. At first, only folks who have spent a lot of time around him would ever see the changes. It is becoming more difficult for him to preach. It seems he cannot gather his thoughts. Occasionally you would overhear someone say, not with malice but with concern, "What's wrong with the pastor?"

A few months before the beginning of his failing health, he became almost obsessed with a massive remodeling project. He was determined to build a large facility. He was so determined that a preliminary draft of a blueprint was drawn. A set of blueprints that were nowhere near completion but somehow my oldest brother, who was a general contractor, convinced the Building and Codes Department in Montgomery County, to approve at least the beginning of the project.

With a $50,000 loan obtained by myself, my brother, and the trustees, the footings were dug and poured and some outside walls would go up. In the early part of 2000, our little congregation did not realize that this would be one of the most tumultuous years of our church's history. My wife and I did not know it at the time, but the Winds of Change were beginning to blow. The church had stepped into the most difficult ride of its 40-year history.

Chapter 18

"Honor Where Honor Is Due"

I recently read a quote from a writer that captured my attention. It was a simple quote but very prolific. It went something like this *"Men and women of God are like candles, they are spent so others can have light."* I have found this to be true. I have seen this by observing and personally knowing church leaders, Sunday school teachers, pastors, evangelists, missionaries, and a vast array of ministers. Dedicated children of God, who devote their lives to serving others.

I've had great respect and will always admire those who encouraged me in my walk with God. The people who influenced me and loved me into the kingdom of God. Many prayed for me and kept showing me not just in words, but in deed also that I was worth something even in my physical condition. That the Lord had a purpose for me. Even a cripple could be a light for others to find their way.

In the Bible, we read about those who have received a calling from God. The Lord speaks to them about their place in His Kingdom. I believe these callings or divine instructions are still prevalent among God's people. I also believe that the Visions or burdens of the Lord cannot be taken lightly. People of God are still moved by his Spirit to reach out to the Lost. I have felt an unction to move from my comfort zone and step out on faith to accomplish something that would help to enhance His Kingdom.

When these desires come over us to be a part of something much bigger than we are, it is a feeling of jubilation, not a feeling of surrender. The attitude of *not my will but yours, Lord.* The determination to step out by faith, with an open heart, and a mind made up to reach for the peace and satisfaction of knowing that our sole purpose is to be pleasing to God. Casting aside all doubt fully trusting. I believe the scripture calls this Faith. *"Now Faith is the substance of things hoped for the evidence of things not seen,"* *Hebrews 11:1.*

In the year 2000, I was a miserable man. That's right, miserable. Burdened, Confused, Conflicted, and seeking Direction. The church I grew up in was struggling. Our man of God, our Mentor, our Father in the Lord, is fighting for his life. The preacher who has performed weddings for our children, preached funerals for our families, stood in the pulpit, and offered encouragement week in and week out for 40 years is slipping away.

The servant who had come to our rescue, the one who has taken our burdens upon himself. The man of God that I have witnessed fasting and praying for the lost, now needs help himself. His faithful congregation is walking around with a deer-in-the-headlights look. How can one man be so important? How can one man's physical condition affect so many people?

During this time of distress, I had been thrust into a more prominent role. As a minister who's been at the church for many years, my duties have increased tremendously. The church was praying and seeking God, looking for direction. Ministers around the country were supportive. The man of God's family was doing everything they could to help during this time. All I needed to do was work and pray and believe everything was going to be alright. I'm still working as a traveling building supply salesman. My customers are many miles away in all directions. My church was 15 miles away in the opposite direction.

I made a committment to prayer. I would get up every morning at 5:00 a.m. and drive from my home in Henrietta to Clarksville. I would pray for at least an hour and then drive the 30 miles to my work base of operation. In my mind and my heart, I was thinking something had to give. Let me stop right here and try to explain something to those who may ask us why we would be so concerned because the church was not going so well.

Holy Ghost-filled Pentecostals live for church. Not just the Fellowship of the Saints, which is important but it's not the most important thing we do in church or at church. We live for the moving of the Spirit. We live for the anointing that comes with those moves. Our strength is renewed week by week by His word. Living for God is not just a lifestyle for us, it is our way of life. So if the Gathering together of his people is jeopardized or threatened in any way through a loss of leadership or by division of any sort, WE PRAY!!!

I must go on and say something here that I believe every saint of God should hear. Many who cry "Lord" and claim to be supportive of a church or a body of Believers are not always what they seem to be. Wolves in sheep's clothing. As word spread around the country that the man of God's health was failing, ministers began to come out of the woodwork. Some were sincere and genuine. Others were opportunists ready to pounce into a position that they had no stake in. Looking for a position without a burden.

Our pastor had a Godly reputation. Our congregation was not that large but it was made up of many people that had been dug out of the ditches of sin. Faithful in every way. A good strong church led up until this point, by a good strong leader. The man of God, his family, and the congregation were facing the challenge of a lifetime. The man of God had symptoms of the early stages of Alzheimer's.

Chapter 19

The Pastoral Years

I n the last days of the year 2000, my life would take a turn that I never really expected. The church that I had attended since I was a child needed a pastor. The founding pastor had become very ill and had entered a long-term nursing care facility. Through an agreement with him and the church body, I stepped into the role of Pastor.

This was something very new. I began to learn that it would be the most challenging time of my life. I am now 47 years old. My wife is the same age, only a few months younger than me. There were not many conversations between my wife and me concerning the decision to go into the unknown future. The future of becoming servants to a congregation of people that had lost their leader. Many of them had faithfully followed this man for many years. A good faithful congregation who truly loved God and His work.

My wife and I had stepped into a work that was much bigger than ourselves, not knowing what the future would hold for us. At this time, in the spring of 2001, the church was right in the middle of a major renovation. The project was barely out of the ground. Looking back to the stage that the building was in at this time, I now realize it truly was a miracle in the making.

My oldest brother, Arthur, had signed on as the general contractor. He was responsible to the city inspectors with building and codes. To put it in plain English he signed up for a passel of headaches and a whole lot of heartaches. He was a generous man and had spent money and time to get the structure out of the ground. We had at this time raised two-story walls around an existing 40-year-old building. I remember a preacher coming during this phase of construction and he described it perfectly. He looked at me and said, *"Well it looks like a church, inside of a church, inside of a church."* We had raised concrete block walls around the old building. We often said it reminded us of the Alamo.

The plan was to put a massive truss roof system over the top of the existing structure. This had to be done without a complete set of blueprints. We only had a blueprint that gave us an architect's rendition of the outside. The inside was planned as we went, and believe me, it took a lot of planning. I'm talking about hair-pulling, head-scratching planning. Situations that were found to be problematic and daily.

Thankfully, as I have already mentioned I was raised in construction. Four brothers, all contractors. Not only that, we had contractors in the congregation who were willing to offer their experience and expertise. The congregation at this time was somewhere around 50 people. Hard-working, faithful people with lots of faith. Many believed in Miracles and we had many milestone miracles on the way.

Many years ago I heard a comedian tell a story about a young high school student, by the name of Leroy. The coach of the local high school football team had his eye on Leroy. Leroy didn't know much about football but the coach had spotted this 250 lb giant. The coach drafted this young man who had the potential to be, in his mind, his star player. They dressed this new addition up in a brand-new uniform. Dressed him in the school colors, looking sharp. The school band is playing, the crowd is roaring. This was a big game.

We had a chance now. We've got a Goliath, a secret weapon. The coach decided he was going to save this secret weapon for a little later in the game. Leroy sat on the sidelines and watched as his teammates were tackled and hit. Driven into the ground. Some were hit so hard that they had to be taken off the field on stretchers. As Leroy sat watching all the horror unfold, the crowd began to chant, louder and louder. *Give the ball to Leroy. Give the ball to Leroy.* Over and over, louder and louder, *Give the ball to Leroy!* All of a sudden Leroy stands up. Hands in the air. Commanding silence from the crowd. He opened his mouth and made a simple five-word statement that went something like this, *"Leroy doesn't want that ball."*

I told you that story to help you understand that I inherited a job that I did not ask for but I knew from the start it was God's will for my life. A new season. A new mission for the church. For my oldest brother and my family. A new day. A new year, 2001, the year of 9/11. The nation would go to war. It was no comparison to the battles that our men and women were fighting on the battlefield. Still, the people at home were fighting their own share of battles. Soldiers, men, and women, out of our congregation were being deployed to fight for our freedom.

During this time and for years to come, we were in the middle of a massive remodeling program. Before it was over, there would be 27,000 sq. ft of Sunday School classes, fellowship hall, prayer rooms, nine restrooms, and an auditorium that would seat 300 people. We jumped into the middle of a dream that would last five and a half years.

When my wife and I took the reins, so to speak, I had left a very good-paying job to take a position that didn't have a guaranteed salary. It felt right. We had prayed about it. I knew I would never fill our former pastor's shoes, only his position. That honor and position I took very seriously at this time. The church had no money. That's right, no construction fund. But we had faith and a bunch of willing workers. Five and a half years later, the project was completed. By God's goodness and mercy and a lot of willing hearts, after spending almost $850,000, the building was ours, Paid in Full, No Debt.

After about 6 years as a pastor, 16-hour days were beginning to take a toll on us, especially my wife. Through all the tear-out and remodeling, which she was always in the middle of, doing more than her share, she began to have breathing problems. The dust and debris from the construction caused massive breathing issues for her. After many visits to a lung specialist, it was determined she was suffering from asthma. For the next two years or more, she was in and out of the hospital. Sometimes for a week or more. It was a trying time for her physically. At this time we still had a church to pastor. By this time we were both in our fifties and struggling. I'm not here to suggest that our life was more difficult than anyone else's. We are now about halfway through our tenure as pastor but we did not know that.

We were installing carpet in our brand-new auditorium when my father came in and sat down on a roll of carpet. Approximately 6 years before, he had come to the church one day as I was working by myself. I was out behind the building picking up about 200 bricks that had been left lying around on the property. I'm not sure why they were there because we were nowhere near ready for any brick. Nevertheless, I did not want to see them go to waste.

The man that I had sat under for 30 years did not waste anything. I moved the bricks away from the building and stacked them up so they wouldn't be in the way. Those bricks were about the same color as the brick we used on the entire building. When the Bricklayers were finishing the building, I had them scatter these approximately 200 bricks in the back wall. I can still point them out, although most people would not know that they are in the wall.

*W*hile I was working my father pulled up in a little Toyota truck. He got out and came over to me and said, *"Ricky don't try to finish this building."* I said to him, *"We're going to finish it with the help of the Lord."* I thought of that conversation as he sat there looking around at an almost completed task and I'll never forget what he said to me. He said, *"Well it looks like you've done it."* At this time my father was dying of cancer. Not long after this conversation, we buried our father.

The church was growing considerably. New families were coming. Ministers were joining the congregation and helping out with preaching and teaching on occasion. We have praise singers, musicians, Sunday School teachers, children's church, etc. Everything is running along pretty well. A new building that the congregation was very proud of and excited about. We still had our day-to-day problems but they were nothing compared to the storms we had weathered.

The long hours and stress were getting to me more than I realized. In 2007 I began to feel bad. I knew it was more than being tired. This is going to be pretty graphic but I started passing blood in my urine. I knew something was wrong. I went to a urologist and discovered that I had bladder cancer. With about a year of treatments and having tumors removed, I was according to my doctor, cancer free. I was so happy but I am now self-cathing. This would go on for the next 10 years. After approximately 3 years, with a cancer-free diagnosis, in 2010 I was informed that the cancer had returned.

My wife and I and our family started making plans to step down from pastoring. After treatments, I was again declared cancer-free but physically I was drained. It was time to resign and allow someone else to step into the office of pastor.

In September 2012, the church voted for a new pastor. It looked like things were still moving forward. My wife and I bought a small condo in another city and began to attend church with my Uncle Jack Batson at New Life Apostolic in Nashville, Tennessee.

Chapter 20

Identity Crisis

*A*t retirement age how do we start over? My father had a saying when we were young and I helped him build houses. At times we would make mistakes and he would say to us, "*Listen, boys, the only man that never makes a mistake is a man that never does anything.*" He was telling us mistakes were not mistakes if we learn from them. So what now? Do we spend the rest of our lives brooding over what should have been? Thinking about the wrong turn we made in the past. Regrets that are plaguing us. Spending our days and nights with thoughts of, if only? If only I had done this or that. If only I could do it all over again. Wallowing in self-pity. Agonizing over circumstances that I cannot control. I am old enough to understand some of the enemy's tactics. I was having a revelation. I knew if the old devil could bog me down and somehow wrap his ugly cloak of disappointment and self-pity around me, I would continue to live in self-blame and discontent.

I no longer held any position of authority. I was no longer the pastor or the business owner as I had been in my younger years. I did not bask in the spotlight of being the top salesman in the company that I had worked in for 10 years. No prestige, no title, no job description. Hardly any phone calls from old cohorts, from saints that we pastored. Very few connections from the past.

Where did all my friends go? Were they my friends? Those ministers who had preached in my Pulpit by invitation, even some not by invitation. Preachers that I allowed to preach as a common courtesy among the brethren. What happened to most of them?

Then I began to realize that life is not about our titles or positions. Life is really about when all of the prestige is stripped away from us. The outer layer is removed when the facade is pulled away. What are we when it is just you and your God? When it's just between you and him?

So I find myself in bed at night brooding about the turns my life has taken. A message that I heard kept coming back to me. I don't know about you but with me, there have been messages or sermons that I have heard and always remembered. This particular sermon by a minister by the name of Billy McCool was not complicated. A simple message titled, *"When you don't know where you are, God knows where you are."*

For those who are reading this, I know it's difficult to understand the gravity of a preacher's dilemma. In my battle with desire versus ability, that desire to preach, to teach, and to witness never left me, but the opportunities were few. I felt like I was on my isle of Patmos. My precious wife and children watched me as I suffered a loss as crucial as the loss of a loved one. I found myself believing everyone had turned against me or almost everyone.

*W*ho wants an old crippled preacher? By this time my health was not good. The cancer had taken its toll on me. I was struggling physically. Tired most of the time. I was taking antibiotics regularly. Infections were a constant threat. Two times a year I was going through cancer screening. On three different occasions, I had been told that the battle was over only to be disappointed to find out the cancer had returned. I had seen the miraculous power of God work, not just in my life but in the lives of others. This disease had hit me so hard. I was having a hard time with my faith. It was a constant battle between faith versus fear.

Maybe my story can help someone else. I was not going to let this trial define who I am or who I could be. I started reaching for the only thing that I knew was solid. That Solid Rock was the word of God. I will never leave you or forsake you.

We have heard people say, *"What doesn't kill you will make you stronger."* I am not sure this is always true. It might strengthen us in character or it may strengthen us spiritually but physically what doesn't kill us can make us weak.

I've heard preaching all of my life about God opening and closing doors. I heard an honest preacher say one time, *"When God closes the door sometimes we are stuck in the hallway."* I'm going to be very blunt here and finish his quote. Please forgive the language but I'll put it the way he did, *"sometimes it is hell in the hallway."* The hallway is full of Doubts, Confusion, Trials, and Tests that we must go through.

Chapter 21

Still Wouldn't Take Anything for My Journey Now

Not one time in my life have I ever doubted the saving power of God. Not one time have I ever said, *"I do not want to live for Him."* Even in times of doubt and confusion, I have never believed that turning away from the Lord was the answer. I was sure that a strong belief in God would carry me through any trial or test. As I had read in the scripture and observed the lives of those who have successfully fought a good fight and kept the faith, I knew that I could make it.

It is now 2013. My wife and I have spent our lives in the work of the ministry and the raising of our children. The pastoral part of our lives was behind us. God has richly blessed us through the years. We had learned to manage our finances. I've always taught and believed that managing money is not just about money but more about behavior.

Fortunately for us, fancy things never appealed to us very much. Don't get me wrong, we had wants like anyone else but our wants were not so extravagant. My wife was not into high-end purses or dresses. We did not and still do not wear jewelry, not even a wedding band. I was never into new automobiles. I've never owned a brand new, no-miles vehicle. I'm certainly not condemning anyone who buys a new vehicle, we just chose to not do so. We had lived in four new houses that we had built. We would live in a house for a few years and then sell it. We would then build another one until finally we were able to clear a house, paid for through an array of real estate purchases of buying and selling.

We now find ourselves living in the small town of Pleasant View, Tennessee. We had bought and paid for a condo. Things were going pretty good. It's now time to do a few things we've always wanted to do. I must confess for many years I had a longing to go out West. One of my only vices was that I loved to read stories of the Old West. Cowboys, Indians, buffalo, deep canyons, and high mountains. I longed to see the magnificent Rockies. My favorite Western writer was Louis L'Amour. With over a hundred novels and short stories in print, these stories would take me to places, in my mind, where I had always wanted to go.

My wife and I decided to take the longest road trip ever. We had places to go and things to see. I need to say this before I go any further. We were raised in a very strict Apostolic Church. I'm talking about a church and a pastor who believed in work, work, work. That's pretty much what we did all the time. In an environment where the church was everything.

*L*et me line out a typical week for my wife, myself, and our family as they were growing up. Sunday morning was the bus ministry. We would get up on Sunday Morning, go to the church, get on a church bus, and go around to pick up kids for Sunday School. We would then go to the church and teach Sunday School as we were both Sunday School teachers. After Sunday service we would again get on the church bus and take the kids back to their homes. On Sunday afternoon we would have choir practice and then it was back to the sanctuary for Sunday night prayer meeting. For one hour we would have a prayer meeting and then a Sunday night service. My wife would then teach at the Christian school on Monday thru Friday. We would have a Monday night prayer meeting and then a Wednesday night Bible Study. On Saturday morning we would go back out for the bus ministry. We would visit the kids that we were going to pick up on Sunday morning and then on Saturday night we would go back to the church for youth service. We would then get up on Sunday morning and start all over again. Hey, get this, now and then our pastor would even call an all-night prayer meeting.

I told you all of this to help you understand that it was very unusual for us to take a vacation. After years of pastoring, we were headed on a journey out West. Across the Mighty Mississippi. Taking a journey that many pilgrims had taken. Loaded up in covered wagons, they traveled, looking for a new home.

I'll quickly cover the highlights of that journey. Through the Badlands of South Dakota into the beautiful Yellowstone Park. Watching Old Faithful spew into the sky. Checking out Mount Rushmore, I saw four of our presidents on the side of that Mountain. The Grand Canyon, Monument Valley, Painted Desert, and the Petrified Forest. The Great Salt Lake down through Utah to Tucson. Over to the Alamo, through Texas. Over the Rockies and on and on seeing the Splendor of God's creation. My wife and I needed that. It rejuvenated us. It refreshed us. A time out to find ourselves. It may have even helped to prepare us for some heartaches to come. Heartaches that we never saw coming.

Not only have we seen the West but we have felt the spray of the Magnificent Niagara Falls in Buffalo, New York. We've crossed the tunnels of Chesapeake Bay. Toured the city of Washington, DC. Observed The Changing of the

Guard at the Tomb of the Unknown Soldier. Saw the gleaming white stones of Arlington National Cemetery. The House of the President and the Capitol Dome. The grave of John F. Kennedy with a flame that still burns today. We've dipped our toes in the Atlantic. Drove through the streets of Charleston and Savannah. Walked on the white sand of the Gulf of Mexico. Many places we've been and had the privilege of seeing cannot be compared to what our Heavenly Father has in store for us in that Holy City, New Jerusalem.

*F*or now, it's back to our condo in Tennessee. We are still here Lord, you must have a purpose. Surely this isn't the end for us.

Chapter 22

Depressed

My oldest brother who we all called Junior, to his business associates and many others he was known as Arthur Reynolds Jr. To those with whom he attended church, he was known as Brother Junior. His employees called him Mr. Reynolds. His children called him dad. His wife called him Honey. Most of the time I affectionately called him Brother.

He was a man of faith with great compassion for those who were not as fortunate. He had a very successful construction company and other business interests.

On September 24th of 2015, he had a birthday party for his wife, Verisa. It was a beautiful party. Lots of laughter and joking around. My brother loved a good clean, leg-slapping joke or story. I would tell him the story of how he was in love with his sixth-grade teacher and how it was a shame that he was so much older than her. He could not tell a joke. He would be laughing so hard that he could not get to the punchline. Sitting at the table laughing and cutting up with him, I had no idea it would be the last time we would speak. I can remember him telling me on the way out, "Thank you for coming." The very next day, Jr and Verisa were getting ready to leave on a cruise for Verisa's birthday and their anniversary.

We received a call that evening. The person on the other end of the line was frantic to the point of being hysterical. It was our sister-in-law, Verisa. Jr had been outside on the tractor moving some brush, getting things ready to leave the next morning. Verisa could not hear the tractor and when she went outside she had not been able to find my brother. *"I don't know where he's at. He was on the tractor working in the yard but I no longer can hear the tractor. I can't find him."*

*T*hey lived in what some would consider a mansion. Their house sat on a bluff overlooking the Cumberland River. Somehow he had gotten too close to the edge of the bluff and went over. He had plunged to the bottom of the bluff. The brother that I loved so dearly was gone. We're all in a daze. His wife, his children, grandchildren, his friends, and his family are all in utter disbelief. More than a loss, this was a tragedy.

After a beautiful funeral with hundreds and hundreds of mourners and friends paying their respects, the reality begins to set in. How was his dear wife going to pick up the pieces? Many properties and construction projects had to be finished without him to help and oversee. A great loss for everyone.

I had lost my father in 2004. My mother had a massive stroke in 2006 and passed away approximately 7 days later. My brother Kenneth had passed away after battling many years of alcoholism. My nephew, Tennion, had drowned while swimming at Harpeth River. We had lost our nephew, Phillip, who was born with Spina Bifida. We then lost our brother Timmy approximately two years after the passing of Jr.

Although we have seen so much loss in our family, for some reason the loss of my brother Jr seemed to have hit us the hardest. At least that was the way it was for me. I went into a deep depression that lasted for many months. I believe there are losses that we never truly get over. All we can hope is that the hurt will not always be so prevalent.

In 2017, I had gone back to my urologist to be told that my cancer had returned. It was at this time that my doctor told me it would take weeks of chemo therapy and radiation to treat the cancer with no promise that it wouldn't be a cure or that it wouldn't return. The other option was to completely remove my bladder. In March of 2017, I went into Skyline Medical Center, in Nashville, and had my bladder removed and a urostomy performed.

Chapter 23

69 Years Old- Back To High School

*I*t is now the end of 2022. Two days before Christmas. I'm preparing for a journey that would be another difficult challenge. The COVID pandemic in the world was beginning to subside. Over 1 million Americans had died because of this dreaded plague. Several of our friends and loved ones had gone on to their eternal reward. There have been major social and economic changes in America and around the world. In all of my time on Earth, I had never seen anything like it.

Social distancing was initiated in just about every place where people normally gathered. Many retail stores and restaurants closed their doors for good. Schools weren't able to be in session.

Our youngest daughter, Misti, was working in the local school system of Clarksville Montgomery County Schools. Her job because of the pandemic closings, was to work in what became known as *Virtual School*. School must continue across America. School systems begin to enact a means for students to learn and live as normal as possible. My daughter and others encouraged me to finish high school. I was very apprehensive at first but I was convinced that this was something I had always longed to do.

Me not being very tech-savvy, I was concerned about being able to understand the ins and outs of using a computer. Technically I was in the Dark Ages. My experience with computers was very limited. The email was something I had never personally used. When I started back to high school at the age of 69 it created quite a stir that I was not expecting. My wife was more technically advanced. She had been using a smartphone and had become very adept at using social media. I had been using a flip phone for many years, mainly for calls. Now I must step up, an old dog needs to learn some new tricks.

I switched to a smartphone. Welcome to the 21st century. I now have an email account. Google has become my new best friend. My new BFF!! The courses I'm having to take are bonafide high school courses. Before my accident, I had only finished the ninth grade. I needed 11 1/2 credits before I could go through the line and graduate with my teenage classmates.

Two days before Christmas, my wife and daughter have gotten me all fixed up and ready to learn. I had a long way to go. English was my most dreaded subject. Judy, my counselor, was very encouraging. My teachers were now sending me emails with words of encouragement. My almost-70-year-old brain was trying to comprehend so much, so fast. I felt like my head was going to explode. How am I ever going to grasp all this?

I am now looking at finishing three years of high school in approximately five months, if I were to go through the line and graduate in May of 2023. I was going to have to work six days a week, five to eight hours a day. English, Business, Music, History, plus other courses that I needed to graduate. I don't know how many times the story of how to eat an elephant went through my head. Do you know how to eat an elephant? One bite at a time. It wasn't all hard work. Some subjects I enjoyed.

My favorite subjects were American and World History. When one of my grandchildren found out that my favorite subject was history, Bailey said to me *"Well granddaddy, that should have been easy, didn't you live through most of it?"* I replied, *"Well I did live through a lot of it."* Sometime in April of 2023, I finished all of my courses. I received the wonderful news from the school that I would graduate with the class of 2023 at the Austin Peay Dunn Center where high school graduations were held.

Chapter 24

Graduation Day

*I*t is the 24th day of May in the year 2023. I can't remember a time in my life when I was as nervous as I am today. I have stood before a congregation hundreds of times both speaking and singing. On many occasions while in business, I have communicated with CEOs, managers, and customers to close large business deals.

Today, three months before my 70th birthday, I'm going before thousands of people, in a large gymnasium, to graduate from high school. My unusual high school graduation has been on social media for several weeks. I have received hundreds of congratulations from people that I did not know.

I won't deny that I have a little bit of anxiety. A news station out of Nashville has been following my story. Chris Davis and Nick Beres, from Channel 5, have already included some short segments in their broadcasts before today. Chris Davis and his cameraman are here at my home to interview me. When the interview is finished we will all be going to the actual graduation. Chris Davis and the cameraman will be there to cover the whole graduation exercise.

I have been wired up with a cordless lapel microphone. Because of my inability to walk long distances, I will be going through the line in a wheelchair. My business teacher, Paul, will be pushing me.

I would be the first of the students to go into the gymnasium behind the teachers and staff. It was very strange to me to be in a long corridor with my teenage classmates who were preparing to walk behind me. The teachers and staff are in the hallway counting down the minutes before the music starts.

They are encouraging and also inspecting the graduate's gowns and hats for Perfection. It's almost time now. We hear *Pomp and Circumstance* as it begins to play. Let's go!! We begin our walk out of the corridor, to be welcomed by thousands of parents, siblings, friends, relatives, loved ones, and dignitaries from the school system. Smiles of achievement on so many faces. I glance up onto the balcony to see my *Three Girls, my Wife of 50 years, my Grandchildren, my Sister, and my Friend*s clapping and smiling for me.

After the pledge. After the welcome speeches. After the students' remarks. All of a sudden I hear my name being called, *Joseph Ricky Reynolds.* I could hear the clapping from the students and the cheering from the balcony by my friends and family.

Channel 5 played the segment on TV many times for the next couple of days. It was never my intention to draw so much attention to myself but it did inspire those that thought it was too late to get their high school diploma. I received an email informing me that the enrollment for the years 23-24 was up more than ever before.

*M*any thanks to my family, friends, teachers, and staff for giving me one of the greatest experiences of my life. I have my diploma hanging on the wall next to my wife's diploma. Ironically, she graduated on the same day 51 years earlier. A diploma is one thing that no one can ever take away from you.

Joseph Ricky Reynolds, Class of 2023

Chapter 25

The Conclusion of the Matter

*T*he preacher, as some may refer to Solomon, wrote in Ecclesiastes Chapter 12 verse 13, *"Let us hear the conclusion of the whole matter; Fear God, and keep his Commandments: for this is the whole duty of man."* My favorite scripture is found in Philippians Chapter 4 verse 13, *"I can do all things through Christ which strengtheneth me."*

Christ is the solid rock on which I stand. I hope and pray that my story of redemption will encourage someone. That my story would help someone realize that it is never too late to change direction. I know looking back at some of my family's history that I would have taken a dead-end road if the Lord had not had mercy on me beside a body of water in Tennessee.

*T*hat day I started a journey that forever changed my life. I know that many who may read my story can look back on their own lives and possibly recall an event or a circumstance that could have changed the course of their lives. The kind word of a stranger reaching out to help. The right word for you at the right time. The kindness and the goodness of God shining through someone that will light up your path for the future.

I promised God as a teenager if he would let me walk again that I would serve him. Looking back it was so foolish to think that I could negotiate some kind of deal with God. I have learned by living for Him for over fifty years that his ways are not my ways.

My desire now, regardless of my circumstances, is to forever be in His will. It took a serious accident to get my attention but I can say, *"I don't regret a mile that I've traveled for the Lord and I don't regret the times I've trusted in his word."* May God richly bless you.

Joseph Ricky Reynolds